Praise for
WOMEN IN POWER

"Erica Combs is a woman of integrity, strength and power. She has the ability to teach people how to create more and let go of what holds them back. *Women In Power* is a must read for anyone wanting to achieve the life of their dreams."
—Susan Sly, *president and CEO, Step Into Your Power Productions LTD., author, speaker, entrepreneur*

"*Women in Power* is an inspirational, empowering book. Erica Combs knows what it takes to be a successful woman in free enterprise today, and she has a unique gift for communicating it to others. If you are looking for an authentic way to live life on your terms and operate from your power, *Women in Power* is a book you'll definitely want to read – and reread!"
—Claudia Volkman, *owner, Creative Editorial Services*

"Astonishing…This book is an absolute delight. Any woman seeking to come into her power should have this book by her nightstand. Read it at night, read it in the morning, and read it when you feel 'resistance.'"
—Ellie Drake, *president, www.BraveHeartProductions.com*

"Erica Combs embodies and exudes the essential ingredients that each Entrepreneurial Woman deserves to uncover within themselves. She is a true example of a Woman in Power!"
—Jamie Mattock, *cofounder, FlowMotion Inc., www.FlowMotionInc.com*

"*Women In Power: a Woman's Guide to Free Enterprise* is by far one of the most powerful books for women in the marketplace today! It has empowered me to take a strong place in business as a woman! It is guiding me to allow my brilliance, radiance, and talents show everywhere I go. Just being in the presence of Erica Combs causes you to rise up to another level in power! I strongly urge you if you truly desire a life of empowerment, to get your hands on this book immediately!"
—Missi Worcester, *president, Dynamic Persona, Inc.*

"You owe it to yourself to read *Women in Power*. You will learn to better understand not only Free Enterprise but also yourself, enabling you to move forward in your business."
—Patti Cornette, *president, Let's Connect Enterprises, wwwLetsConnectEnterprises.com*

Praise for WOMEN IN POWER

"I want to thank Erica Combs from my heart for being a pioneer of Women in Power! She is a true woman who knows her power. She truly exercises her creativity through talent and heart to reach out to all women and all people to pave this trusting path where we can all learn that it is ok to be human and to receive good treasures that are beyond material things. Thank you so much again, and I reach out to you from my heart in sincere gratitude to you."   —Marisol Gutierrez, *entrepreneur*

"It is rare to find a book that offers both insight and practical guidance. Erica is an inspiration to all who seek true personal growth."   —Shirley DiPace, *entrepreneur*

"Erica has replaced my doubts with renewed confidence, my indecisiveness with an ability to make right decisions in minutes, to strive for more and obtain it, to have that inner knowing what I want and to not only ask for it but believe in my worthiness to receive. (I am 57 years of age and many of these changes are happening in me for the very first time!) Erica Combs is so much more than a voice that encourages you. She's truly a cocreator with you in achieving the dreams and desires of your life!"
                                                              —Beverly G. Ameykeller

WOMEN IN POWER

WOMAN'S GUIDE TO FREE ENTERPRISE

ERICA COMBS

ISBN: 0-9740924-3-6

More Heart Than Talent Publishing, Inc.

6507 Pacific Ave #329
Stockton, CA 95207 USA
Toll Free: 800-208-2260
www.MoreHeartThanTalentPublishing.com

FAX: 209-467-3260

www.WomenInPower.net

Cover art by FlowMotion Inc.

ACKNOWLEDGEMENTS

I have desired to become an entrepreneur my entire life. It is my privilege to be living my dream as a speaker, author, and mentor. My life has been an incredible journey thus far, filled with challenges and triumphs, emotional breakthroughs and many learning experiences before finally reconnecting with my power and my self-esteem. Free Enterprise is a remarkable opportunity to grow and to change, and it has allowed me to give myself the permission to be the brilliant person I have always dreamed of being.

There is a very special group of people who have assisted me through this process and have encouraged me to keep reaching for my dreams when I required their support.

My heartfelt thanks to my husband Jeffery Combs who has believed in my brilliance and more importantly, my heart since the day we met. I could not have completed this project without his support and encouragement, but most importantly, his love. His absolute faith in me and his consistent support have created the foundation for me to step into my power and share my story to assist others.

I also thank my editor Claudia Volkman for her encouragement, energy, and skill to bring my ideas to reality.

I would like to thank Jamie Mattock and her husband Christopher for all of their support and their contributions of the cover design, book layout and artwork, and for all of their collaborations.

And finally, but most importantly, I thank my mom and dad for always believing in my greatness and for supporting me through my times of challenge as well as those of triumph. This book would have never taken place without their love and their valuable contributions in my life.

WOMEN IN POWER

CONTENTS

FOREWORD

It is my absolute pleasure to introduce you to an individual who will assist you to speed up your transformation process. I have had the fortune of knowing Erica in many capacities. She has been my student, friend, business partner, and loving wife. The quality I admire most in Erica is that she lives what she speaks and teaches. She has an extraordinary ability to intuitively see and feel other people's pain and then deliver the insight that will allow them to release their pain and begin their transformation from a perspective of power rather than anxiety.

Erica's keen insight comes from her victories in understanding the emotions that drove her to numerous addictions. The ability to deliver her message from what she has learned and is learning is what creates her uniqueness. Reading this book will empower you to wake up and come alive in a whole new way as Erica assists you to understand the causes that continue to drive your effects.

As you read this book, allow yourself to come from the power in your vulnerability so that you may live more in your heart and less in your analytical mind. Erica is a voice that you deserve to receive on your journey to your prosperous promised land.

Jeffery Combs
President, Golden Mastermind Seminars, Inc.
www.GoldenMastermind.com

WOMEN IN POWER

INTRODUCTION

Whether you are already a successful entrepreneur, just beginning a new venture, or simply romancing the vision of owning your own business one day, this book will greatly assist you to understand how to win the game of free enterprise.

My vision of this book began in October, 2004 when I was seeking information specifically designed for entrepreneurial women. I found plenty of information about how to climb the corporate ladder and many books for women with jobs or seeking them, but could not find any information about women in free enterprise.

Rather than feeling frustrated by this situation, I became inspired. I saw an opportunity to bring value to the marketplace and decided to create a forum for women to connect and collaborate. I am passionate and committed to assisting people, especially women, to change the way they feel in order to achieve their goals and dreams. It is my desire to see women step into the limelight of free enterprise and receive the results and recognition they not only desire, but absolutely deserve.

The seven million dollar question is "How do I succeed in free enterprise?" I can assure you firsthand through my entrepreneurial experience since 1996 that success as an entrepreneur requires an entirely different level of self-esteem, communication, focus, and permission than most women are taught is acceptable by their families, coworkers, and peers.

Success requires that you begin to examine your current beliefs and give yourself permission to release those that no longer serve you so you can adopt new and empowering beliefs to lead you to manifesting your dreams.

The purpose of this book is to create a foundation for you to begin your journey to personal power, and to create an anchor you can use to reconnect with your internal peace as you continue your journey of personal development in the land of free enterprise. In my experience, the productivity and expansion of any enterprise is a direct reflection of the personal growth achieved by the person responsible for the business. This is why I believe it is imperative that we learn to neutralize and release the negative emotions and chaos that take us out of peace and out of our power. You see, your power is your peace, and your peace comes from how comfortable you are with you. When you are at ease with your mind, body, and spirit, then you are in your power!

There are many gifts inside this book for you to receive to assist you on this journey. I welcome you to connect with me at www.WomenInPower.net and actively participate with me to create a culture to support Women In Power. Together, we can create a team of strong, powerful, peaceful entrepreneurs focused on achieving a higher level of consciousness, success, and peace in free enterprise. I look forward to receiving your message and having the opportunity to connect with you and to assist you in your entrepreneurial transformation!

www. WOMENinPOWER.com

I invite you to actively participate with me to create a culture to support entrepreneurial women worldwide. The Women in Power website will provide you with valuable resources and connections created to assist you as you build your enterprise and expand your personal power.

To celebrate the success of entrepreneurial women in free enterprise, I'd like to invite you to share your personal stories with other powerful women. What kind of an impact has Women in Power had on you, and what insights did you gain from your reading? How has what you read made a difference in the way you approach your business?

Contact me directly at www. WomenInPower.com to receive a free gift I have created for you to use each and every day to reaffirm your power to create the peace and self-acceptance you have always desired and absolutely deserve!

Women In Power Unite!

1

POWER

What is power? If you are reading this book, it is because you desire more power in your life. But what is power? Is it influence over others? Is it the ability to be a strong and inspiring leader? Is power an attribute we possess naturally at birth, or is it acquired during a lifetime? This book will greatly assist you in your journey of personal development and entrepreneurial success by helping you to understand what power is, why it is imperative to find *your* power, and then how to use your power to leverage yourself in the game of free enterprise.

Developing Emotional Autonomy

My personal definition of power is *developing emotional autonomy*. This may sound very scientific to you, but emotional autonomy is just another way of saying *emotional independence*. Emotional independence is crucial to success in any endeavor involving other people. Consider this for a moment. Are you really willing to build your career based on how other people feel? Or are you ready to succeed, even if your success contradicts someone else's struggle?

Unless you are selling coconuts to yourself on an island you will require interaction with other people to create a flourishing business. As a business owner, you cannot afford to base the success of your enterprise on the current emotional state of the people you are doing business with! If someone else is having a bad day or a negative experience in the exact moment you happen to call on them, realize that you are not responsible for their current situation. You are also under no obligation to begin to resonate with them in their current emotional state if it is lower than yours. This is all about energy. If you are feeling great, your energy is high, and all is well in your world, it is not your responsibility to make sure everyone else's life is flowing like yours! In business you will find people having bad days, great days, so-so days, up days, down days, and a plethora of other emotional experiences. Instead, it is your responsibility as a business owner to allow yourself to stay focused in the present moment, unaffected by the emotions of those around you.

Is this a daunting task? It can seem like one if you are already looking at your entire life and everyone you do business with and thinking, *This is overwhelming.* Objectivity and responsibility are two of the most empowering situations you can ever allow yourself to experience. This is why each of these topics has received its own chapter in this book. I will tell you now, however, that objectivity simply means "the release of negative emotion" and responsibility means "the ability to respond."

If you are seeking to impact and affect other people through your product or service, then it is imperative that you begin to develop enough emotional resiliency that you can stay in your power and remain emotionally independent of the emotions of the people around you. Otherwise, you will find yourself on an emotional roller coaster with no idea when the ride will end! It is far more terrifying to ride the emotions of others that it is to connect with your own.

Consider this for a moment: we live in a society that is just learning how to express emotions verbally. Most of us have been conditioned to assess the emotional state of those around us by paying attention to tone of voice, body language, facial expression, etc. I have a client who learned to judge the emotional state of her father by the way he held and rattled the newspaper! This one simple situation let her know if it was a good day to seek interaction with him. Being in your power means giving yourself permission to feel how YOU feel, and to live your life on your terms, even if this means contradicting the status quo.

When you are in your power, you will find that you have the ability to influence others to take action, to be a strong and inspiring leader; people will begin to gravitate toward you as you resonate with the inner strength and courage they seek to possess. This is where your energy comes in to play. How is your energy on average on a daily basis? Is it fairly high, low, or somewhere in the middle? Do you allow your energy to radiate from you to impact the people around you, or do you suppress it in your body, hoping that no one will notice you?

When I talk about energy, I mean your emotional energy, your etheric energy. This is the energy you project each and every moment in each and every conversation or situation you find yourself in. Usually, this energy is subconscious and you are not even aware of it. It is possible, however, to become conscious of your energy and its projection and to begin affecting the environment around you in a way that allows you to receive the results you seek to create. This is when you begin attracting the people and situations you desire instead of futilely chasing your goals and dreams. If you have ever been around someone charismatic, you know how good you felt in their presence. Charisma is another example of energy projection. It is so much easier to attract what you desire than it is to go and get it. In order to do this, you must begin to be aware of your energy. If you desire good situations such as success, money, great clients and great people you can collaborate with, this will require you to begin to operate from a much higher energetic vibration in your body. This means feeling comfortable being yourself so you can begin feeling good about being *you*.

Your energy is the value you bring to free enterprise. Never before has there been anyone like you in life, and never again will there be anyone like you once you are gone. This is why there is the opportunity for success for everyone who has the courage to engage in entrepreneurship! Regardless of your product or service, what you are really marketing is you. You are marketing the opportunity to connect with you, to collaborate with you, to create results with you. Because you are unique, the only limit to your value in the marketplace is that which you impose on yourself. It is imperative that you begin to understand right now that this game is limitless! You have the opportunity as an entrepreneur to create any and all results you desire. You have the opportunity to live your dreams! Isn't this enough reason to engage in the process of change and personal development? This is going to require that you take some risks. It's a process called "risk for reward." Business is not a lottery, where if you happen across the right numbers, success finds you by chance. Winning the game of business and free enterprise simply means you stay in the process long enough to begin taking bigger risks to receive bigger rewards. Being in the process means that you don't expect yourself to create massive results in your first ninety days in a new endeavor. It means allowing yourself to learn as you continue your journey toward success and it means becoming objective about your results along the way.

Enjoy the Game of Free Enterprise

In reality, free enterprise is very much a game. I have found in our business that the more fun I allow myself to have, the more open I become to creating experiences that I find pleasurable, and the more results I can achieve. Winning this game is not about who holds the best cards at the end of the game, it is about who is creating the most enjoyment as the game is played! This is about the process, and if you are going to succeed as an entrepreneur, you will unequivocally be required to create pleasure within your business. As human beings, we operate from two perspectives: pleasure and pain. That which we perceive to be pleasurable, we do, and that which we perceive to be painful, we resist. This is a basic rule that applies to all of us. In a job, we receive the reward of a paycheck even if we do not particularly enjoy the tasks required to get paid. In a job, compensation is cyclical and we know exactly how much time will pass between paychecks.

As an entrepreneur, it is up to you to create the results which will in turn put money in your bank account. Big results require big action, but not only big action—consistent action. This is why it is imperative that you find a way to create pleasure in your business. If you subconsciously resist producing in your enterprise because you perceive it to be painful, you will find all manner of ways and excuses to sabotage your results. When you are having fun, you feel good, your energy is higher, and you vibrate at a much higher frequency.

This allows you to attract people and situations that resonate with your energetic message.

I used to believe that to run our corporation, I had to be in my office sixteen hours a day. I believed I was required to produce, produce, produce, and when that was over produce some more. I was subconsciously angry about all of this production and was not a lot of fun to be around. I was putting so much emotional pressure on myself to perform perfectly that I created a false perception of reality. There was no joy in what I did because I felt I had to make myself do things I did not enjoy. I believed I had to be chained to my desk and married to our business, and I felt guilty for every moment I spent outside of my office. What a contradiction! The whole point of owning your own business is to create leverage so you can enjoy life! This means being out of the office and experiencing the world! I have learned that success does not require constant productivity. Success requires you to create a game which is so rewarding and emotionally fulfilling that you consistently play it to create consistent rewards. Not constantly play, but *consistently*.

Release the Pressure of Perfection

This is about releasing your emotional pressure to succeed perfectly. There is no such situation as perfect success! Every successful person I have ever connected with has stories about the ups and downs they have experienced on their journey. Let's face it, we all have issues, but you don't have to wait until they are all resolved to create the results you are seeking from life. There is a tremendous amount of power in releasing your expectation of what you can achieve when you are new to business. As a speaker, personal coach, and mentor, I see so many people expecting themselves to achieve tremendous results when they have not developed their skills yet! Being in your power means knowing that as an entrepreneur, you have skills to acquire, lessons to experience, and growth to achieve on your journey in business. It means recognizing that you are exactly where you are supposed to be in life right now, transitioning to where you desire to be. It means accepting that you and your business are masterpieces in progress, and releasing your expectation of what the finished canvas will look like. More importantly, it means not judging yourself or your enterprise for not being perfect.

Power is about acceptance. It is about allowing yourself to see you as you really are without judgment or criticism. If you are reading this book, you and I have something in common. We are both seeking change and development. You see, you don't have to be as successful as I am or have the fame or notoriety of a star to begin connecting and resonating with the people you desire in your enterprise. There is power in the process of growth and change; the key is being able to recognize it. The power you are seeking is there within you just waiting for you to tap into it. My clients all ask me "How do I get in my power?" I always answer this question the same way. I say, "That is a great question, but I have a better one. What keeps you from your power?" If you are not connected with your power, you want to begin asking yourself this question. When you understand the emotions that are creating this situation, you move into a whole different level of awareness as you continue to grow. It is much easier to address your issues when you understand what they are!

Free enterprise is a very simple concept. It is marketing a product or service and receiving compensation in return. It's our internal emotional dialogue which complicates the process. There are two phases of every business: momentum and stability. Most people are so focused on how life will be when their business is stable that they never create any momentum. Realize that creating momentum requires a tremendous amount of consistent energy in the beginning, but always gets easier later in the process. A freight train does not pull out of the station at 70 miles an hour. It requires time and fuel to gradually move from a standstill to a speeding locomotive. Once the train has the right momentum to achieve the desired speed, it requires much less energy to stay stable at that velocity. Your business operates on the same principle. Building momentum in your business on a daily basis is what will one day lead you to stability. This building phase is where most people get stuck. This is where their emotional issues begin to come to the surface. This is also where a tremendous amount of growth is created. Quantum leaps can occur in the momentum stage provided you stay in the process long enough to experience them.

The success you seek in free enterprise is an external expression of power that resonates from within. Have you ever asked anyone who is very powerful where their inspiration and strength comes from? If you do, you will quickly find that they are driven by an internal purpose and passion for the value they know they can bring to life. Perhaps this person is achieving great wealth or bringing new and empowering information to increase the consciousness of our society. Whatever the situation, you will find that they have an unshakeable belief that they have a unique message that will contribute to the greater good of mankind and are willing to journey through the process of short-term sacrifice to achieve a long-term objective. They are willing to remain strong in the face of adversity to reap the rewards that will come in return for the value of their message, product or service.

Remaining strong in the face of adversity means remaining grounded in how you really feel, regardless of the actions or reactions of other people. Adversity does not necessarily have to be a life-altering situation. Adversity can come in the form of a friend or family member who does not share your vision or perhaps is not able to see the same value in your product or service as you do. Regardless of the adversity you may be facing, when you are in your power you will remain emotionally independent of the opinions of the people around you. This means you hear and experience the feedback you receive, but you do not create an emotional connection to this information. It means you remain objective and consider the source of the information you are receiving.

Creating Entrepreneurial Power

So what is entrepreneurial power? It is the choice to begin creating a high energy field within to operate from rather than a low one. You have the power to choose your feelings, language, and reactions, and each of these contribute to your overall level of vibration. Power is choosing to foster the positive rather than attack the negative. Power is understanding that people buy emotionally. Feelings determine purchases and investments. Feelings determine whether someone decides to take advantage of your product or service or keep looking for another opportunity.

When people feel good about you, they are much more likely to buy from you. Power is giving yourself permission to be yourself. It is recognizing your own value and allowing other people to feel good about being in your energy field.

WOMEN IN POWER

Notes

_____

_____

_____

_____

_____

_____

_____

_____

_____

_____

_____

_____

_____

_____

_____

_____

_____

_____

_____

_____

_____

_____

_____

Notes

_____

_____

_____

_____

_____

_____

_____

_____

_____

_____

_____

_____

_____

_____

_____

_____

_____

_____

_____

_____

_____

_____

2

THE POWER OF BELIEF

In my opinion, beliefs are one of the most powerful contributors to entrepreneurial success. Your beliefs about yourself, your business and the marketplace will absolutely impact the results you create. Not only will your beliefs affect your results, they will also determine the reality you live and the situations you experience each and every day. If you desire different results in life than you are receiving or have previously created, it will require you to change your beliefs.

I'm sure you have heard the adage that the definition of insanity is taking the same action again and again, yet expecting different results. We take action based on our beliefs; we also resist taking action based on our beliefs about what may happen. I have found as a personal coach and mentor that many of my clients resist the exact actions that would produce revenue in their businesses because of their beliefs about success and failure. Believe it or not, more people have anxiety regarding success than failure. For most of us, achieving the success we desire conflicts with our struggle, a situation we are very familiar with. The word familiar is derived from the Latin word *familiaris* meaning "that of family." It is within our families that we begin creating our beliefs and perceptions about ourselves and the world around us.

As human beings, we create beliefs based on the emotions connected to events we experience. It is our emotions connected to a particular belief that gives it power. Remember that a belief is merely your perception of an event or situation. You can choose in any given moment to create new and empowering beliefs that serve your current purpose if what you currently hold to be true is not serving you to create the results you desire.

Creating a Life by Design

As you become more conscious about your beliefs, you will begin noticing how they shape your reality. Most people go through the mundane activity of life without ever considering that they can change their circumstances. Their beliefs remain subconscious, and they continue to settle for making a living rather than choosing to design a life. This idea of creating a life by design is very powerful, and this is why it is imperative that you begin to become conscious of your beliefs and your perceptions of the world and yourself. Consciousness means awareness; just by reading this information you are already beginning to pay attention to the emotions, thoughts and ideas that are constantly being created in your mind. Each of us has the power to either create our reality or choose to merely exist. If you are seeking entrepreneurial success, the only person creating the resistance between you and the results you desire is you!

Never underestimate the power of your beliefs. Your interpretation of yourself and the world around you and your expectancy of what will happen in response to your actions absolutely determines the quality of the life you live. This explains the "placebo effect." A placebo effect occurs when improvement in the condition of a sick person cannot be attributed to the specific treatment used. Why? Because the patient believes the treatment will cure their condition even though in this instance, they are only taking a sugar pill containing no medication! Take a moment to realize that your mind can heal you body if it is operating from the proper belief. This is how powerful each and every thought you have ever had about yourself and the world around you is. You are currently living in a reality of your own design. If you desire a different experience, begin to change what you believe.

Take moment to reflect on your beliefs about yourself. Are your beliefs positive and empowering? Keep in mind that a belief is simply an idea that you hold to be true. The power of a belief is based on the amount of certainty you connect to it. So what do you believe to be true about yourself? Take a moment to stop reading and say, "I fully accept myself exactly as I am and feel good about who I am becoming." Whether this statement is a belief that will create your reality or merely a passing thought will depend on how much certainty is attached to it. If you think, *Well, I accept myself most of the time and feel okay about my progress,* what you really mean is, *I don't feel certain that I accept myself and feel food about the changes I am experiencing.* If you do not accept yourself, it will be very difficult to learn to love yourself. This will have a direct impact on your self-esteem and self-confidence. In free enterprise the commodity you are marketing is you, and this will make it very difficult to attract the people, situations, and success that you seek.

A Personal Story

I'm going to take a moment to share with you one of my limiting beliefs and how I was able to change it. Before I met Jeffery in 2002, I had a history of what I call "bad men." These men were not "bad" in the criminal sense, but they were bad for me emotionally through no fault of their own. Because I had a belief that I was not good enough to be lovable, I would create relationships with men who could not love me so that I could reaffirm my belief abut myself. Eventually, these relationships would dissolve and the abandonment I felt as a result continued to validate the certainty I felt about not being lovable. In 2002, I attended a workshop in Columbus, Ohio which unequivocally changed my life forever. I drove 100 miles south of where I lived to attend my first motivational seminar and met Jeff who was the speaker for the day. I connected with Jeff's life story of struggle, addiction, recovery, and success.

During the course of the day I began to believe for the first time in my life that I was lovable despite my imperfections. I went home and decided that day that I deserved a man exactly like Jeff in my life. I decided to attract someone who had overcome some obstacles, someone who was constantly seeking growth, and someone who had the heart to assist other people to grow and develop. I made this decision in a moment and also decided to stop looking for "Mr. Right." I decided to focus on my own growth and development with absolute faith that when I was ready, the perfect man for me would find me. I had no idea when I made these decisions that I would attract Jeff into my life, but in retrospect, each characteristic I declared I deserved is a very apt description of my husband. It is no accident I attracted him. I changed my belief about myself and what I deserved, and this decision began my transformation from average to exceptional. I began this transformation long before Jeff and I began our relationship. My transformation began with one idea, one *belief* about myself and what I deserved.

Your Past Is Your Prologue

I share this with you because no matter where you are in life, no matter what your history is, you can begin creating what you desire right now in this instant. To quote the great playwright William Shakespeare in *The Tempest*, "What's past is prologue." Your past does not have to equal your future. Your history can be perceived as the prologue to today. The rest of your story is yet unwritten. Your life story can begin today, and you can create a story of success and abundance if this is what you desire. All this requires is a decision from you. One decision is all that is required to change your beliefs if they are not serving you. It really is this simple.

Take some time to examine your beliefs about yourself, because these beliefs are the foundation of your reality. Here are a few questions to consider:

How do I feel about myself on a daily basis?
Do I feel guilty about past situations or relationships?
Do I allow my emotions from past situations to affect my decisions in the present?
How do I feel I am perceived by other people?
Do I feel I am a competent businessperson?
Do I feel comfortable in my body?
Do I feel I deserve to receive the success I seek?

Notice all of these questions are based on your current emotional state. This is because each situation you experience in life leads you to create a new belief, based on the emotion you attach to that event. This is true for events from the past, as well as what you are currently experiencing. If you desire a different experience in life, begin changing your beliefs about what life has to offer you. So many people develop limiting beliefs about what they are capable of achieving because they perceive they have failed in the past. My question here is always, "Did you really fail, or did you gain information from an experience?"

Changing Your Beliefs

Changing your beliefs is going to require a different level of objectivity than society teaches us to operate from. We live in a very subjective world where good and bad and right and wrong receive far too much emotional attention. Most people resist objectivity because they associate this word with a lack of emotion. Objectivity is simply the ability to view a situation without judgment. It means releasing the idea of good/bad and right/wrong. Far too often, we equate desirable experiences with being good or taking the "right" action and assign negative emotions to situations that do not unfold as we desire. In any experience, whether the outcome is successful or creates a subsequent challenge, you have the opportunity to grow and learn because of that experience. This involves becoming more objective about life. It means releasing the inclination to judge each situation as a success or a failure. In life, there are no failures. Failure or success is based solely on your perception of reality. This is why one man's trash is another man's treasure. This is why success is like beauty—it is held in the eye of the beholder. Success and failure is different for each person so what you perceive as failure could be perceived as success by someone else.

What beliefs do you currently have about yourself that you are beginning to recognize no longer serve you? It can be very cathartic to create a list called "What I believe to be true" and then evaluate that list for what is empowering and what is disempowering. You can replace any disempowering belief with a new empowering belief in the exact moment you become aware of the disempowering belief and are ready to release it. If you are still skeptical about the power of your beliefs, consider this for a moment. How many times have you received a clue that something bad was going to happen? You think, *Oh God, wait until the other shoe drops.*

I know something bad is going to happen. How often do you perceive that Monday will be a struggle, and Friday will be a breeze? Don't you consistently prove yourself right? This is because you are operating from your beliefs. You attract the exact situations to you which will reaffirm what you already hold to be true. This is why your beliefs are so powerful. Realize that you have the power within you to consciously create all of the experiences you are seeking in life and in business if you begin to believe you can create them.

At this point in gaining awareness about beliefs, many of my clients begin to criticize themselves and "kick" themselves for entertaining the emotions and beliefs they realize are disempowering. If you are doing this too, STOP! Remember objectivity? Your beliefs allowed you to get here. Without them, you would not be reading this information! Instead of judging yourself for your beliefs and emotions, consider being grateful for how they served you. Even if your beliefs have served you imperfectly when it comes to achieving your dreams, consider all of the experience and knowledge you have gained as a result. Doesn't this allow you to have a better understanding of people and of life? Is it possible that your experience will enable you to assist someone else experiencing a similar challenge?

Your past beliefs allowed you to survive until today. If you desire the ability to design your life rather than settle for making a living, what beliefs are you ready to release right now? What beliefs are you ready to create? Here are a few of the beliefs I have embraced on my journey which have allowed me to reconnect with my power and become the person I have always dreamed of being:

I am lovable because I exist.
I deserve to receive all of the good in life I desire.
I am a producer.
I am a leader.
I have value.
I am safe.
I can respond to any situation.
Each moment is a moment of transition.

My past is merely my prologue.
I am a competent businesswoman.
I can create any situation I desire to experience.

Small Shifts Create Quantum Leaps

These beliefs began as a series of affirmations. Over time, I began applying them to my life and then observing how my life changed. Because of this transition, I have a much stronger foundation of what I believe to be true and what I believe I deserve. This is a process. You will not magically wake up one morning with a complete set of inspiring, empowering beliefs which allow you to remake your life in twenty-four hours to live your vision of success. As you release the emotions and beliefs which no longer serve you, you will become aware of other beliefs you never knew existed. Welcome to the journey! Small shifts in consciousness compound to create quantum leaps in life. Napoleon Hill said, "What the mind can conceive and believe, the body can achieve." Give yourself the opportunity to reconnect with your mind before you begin to judge the effectiveness of your new beliefs. Consider how long you have operated from your old belief system. Repetition and experience with your new beliefs will allow you to create the changes you are seeking.

As you go through this process, do not seek the approval or advice of others. Practice your new beliefs with complete disregard to the opinions of others unless they have achieved the success you are seeking. Learn to become you own best sounding board and greatest ally. Realize that other people may predict what you are or are not capable of accomplishing, but only you have the power to create your future!

Notes

_____
_____
_____
_____
_____
_____
_____
_____
_____
_____
_____
_____
_____
_____
_____
_____
_____
_____
_____
_____
_____
_____
_____

Notes

_____

_____

_____

_____

_____

_____

_____

_____

_____

_____

_____

_____

_____

_____

_____

_____

_____

_____

_____

_____

_____

3

THE POWER OF PERMISSION

One of the greatest lessons you will learn as an entrepreneur is that the only permission required to succeed is your own. When you give yourself this permission, you begin to operate from an entirely different level of awareness and approval. I have been very fortunate in my life regarding external approval. My parents always told me I could be and do anything I set my mind to, and they always supported me when I immersed myself in a new endeavor.

In many ways, success has always been easy for me, but keeping the success has been an entirely different challenge. I spent many years of my life vacillating between my brilliance and my feelings of unworthiness. Until I began giving myself permission and approval, I continued this struggle between achievement and sabotage. Internal permission and approval is based on the foundation of feeling lovable, good enough, and deserving of the situations you seek to create through your enterprise.

If you are the first or one of a select few entrepreneurial people in your family, be prepared to accept that your relatives may not understand your venture or your purpose. It is very normal to seek the approval of those who are close to us when we begin a new venture. Just keep in mind that the people who are closest to you may not have the ability right now to see the same vision you do. Success in free enterprise requires a completely different set of rules than any other life experience, and most of society is not going to understand the process you are undertaking to create freedom in your life. After all, isn't emotional, spiritual, financial freedom, or some combination of the three your main motivation for getting started in your enterprise? People who are satisfied in their job with no desire for more will not understand this quest. This does not make them bad people or any less valuable to you. I want to stress here that these are good people. But you are seeking an exceptional life rather than an average one, and this first requires an excellent emotional dialogue with yourself, and a clear understanding of permission, approval, and how to create it for yourself when you are standing alone in your vision.

Permission to Be Unique

Building an enterprise can at times feel very lonely because by having the courage to pursue your dreams, you are headed into uncharted territory. This is why there is so much opportunity in free enterprise. When you begin to manifest your unique vision of a business, realize that no one else has ever had your exact vision. No one else has had your experience, and no one else can deliver your message in the way you can. This comes back to marketing your uniqueness, the value only you bring to the game of life.

In order to capitalize on your unique self, this requires that you give yourself permission to be different from everyone else. This means you begin living in your authentic self. It means you begin allowing people to experience the person you really are inside instead of playing it safe and hiding behind one of the many masks created by your ego. By ego, I don't mean being egotistic or exaggerating your sense of self-importance. I'm not talking about an attitude of "I am an entrepreneur. I am better than you." I define ego as the internal critic which is created as a result of your past experiences. This critic relates to your belief system about yourself and what is required for you to be accepted by others.

Permission to be yourself begins with releasing your emotional attachment to receiving approval from the people around you. It is normal to desire social acceptance and to be liked by the people in your life, but if you find yourself operating differently from one person to the next in order to gain their approval, how much time and energy are you expending making sure you please everyone? If you are fun-loving and boisterous at heart, yet expected to be serious and contemplative and you suppress your innate nature to meet these expectations, how much room do you have left to be creative? If you are anxious about how people expect you to act, what they expect you to be like, and how you should look like once you succeed, how much energy do you have left to take action in the only moment that counts, meaning this one?

In my life, I attended three different high schools from halfway through my sophomore year to when I graduated. In public high school, like everyone else, I sought social acceptance from my peers. The challenge for me was that I was involved in different activities than they were and this inhibited my opportunities to spend time and connect with them. While the other girls were cheerleading, running track, playing volleyball, etc., I was riding my horse and competing in horse shows, which were great experiences for me, but they were so foreign to the other girls in my school that it was challenging to create relationships. The time commitment required for me to achieve the success I sought as an equestrian did not allow for socializing after school or just "hanging out" on the weekends. I went straight from school to the barn, spent three to four hours a day there, and spent all day on Saturdays and Sunday competing. I spent tremendous amounts of time moving from social circle to social circle seeking a group of friends I could connect with. I did not realize at the time that I was creating my own disconnection from my peers, because I spent so much time trying to be like everyone else that I never let anyone get close enough to establish a friendship. The few friendships I did experience I sabotaged. I did not give myself permission to be good enough to receive the love these friends were extending to me, and I subconsciously created arguments and fights to terminate them.

It was not until I went to my first private boarding school to complete the second half of my sophomore year that I began to give myself permission to live in my own uniqueness. Ironically, it was my anger that allowed me to begin connecting with myself. As unhappy as I was in public high school, I did not want to leave home to attend a boarding school. I was so angry to be there that I didn't care what my peers thought of me and didn't invest any energy into being liked or accepted.

For the first time in a social environment, I focused on what I wanted in the situation instead of attempting to fit in with the people around me. This created a tremendous amount of curiosity among my peers, and within two weeks they were approaching me to find out who I was and what I was all about. I then transferred to a different school to complete my last two years of high school. At this point, I was ready to be open and connect with my peers and I created solid relationships which have continued into the present. There is tremendous power and freedom in giving yourself this permission; it is absolutely necessary to tap into your authenticity as an entrepreneur. Permission to market your uniqueness will create the same wave of curiosity in the marketplace as it did among my peers in high school. This will also allow you to begin attracting people to you who seek to experience your value and will accept and respect you exactly as you are.

In this game, you will find that respect is much more valuable than being liked. You will also find that people will accept you because they respect you, even if they do not like you immediately. Just being an entrepreneur is reason enough for some people to decide they do not like you—for no other reason than what you are doing with your life contradicts theirs. It is important that you develop a level of objectivity regarding the feedback you receive from others in business, personal relationships, and life.

To create this objectivity, you must begin to consider the source of the information you are receiving. If a person has not created the success you seek, consider putting their feedback into a category in your mind labeled "For What It's Worth." Realize that if your goals and dreams are bigger than theirs, their feedback may not serve you, so it is important that you do not take it personally, thus allowing them to affect your conviction that you are in the right place at the right time in your enterprise. I have found on my journey that being objective regarding the feedback and comments of others enables me to spend less time being angry or offended by what people say. Let's face it, most of us are not trained to be great communicators and we can offend someone without intending to. But there are often pieces of value within another person's message if you open your mind to viewing their comments objectively.

Permission to Prosper

Creating success in free enterprise also requires that you give yourself permission to prosper. This sounds simple, but have you ever taken a moment to consider your emotional dialogue with money? A great indicator of your money dialogue is the balance in your bank account. It is important to be objective about this observation and realize that today's results are an indication of yesterday's dialogues and, you can begin today to create the results you desire in your enterprise.

Money has a very negative stigma in our society. Somewhere along the way, it has become generally accepted that the rich keep the poor from advancing, that it is not possible to be lovable or to receive love if you are succeeding financially, and that wealthy people have somehow achieved their financial status through some underhanded means. These may not be your personal beliefs, but if you ask almost anyone about money you can observe their negative reaction. Most people do not believe that there is enough money in the world, and they believe it is hoarded by a select few.

Permission to Receive

Prosperity begins with profit, and creating profit in your bank account requires that you become comfortable receiving money. Receiving is intrinsically spiritual whether you are receiving compliments, love, or money. How do you feel when someone offers you a compliment? Are you open to receiving it, knowing that you deserve it or do you deflect the compliment because it makes you uncomfortable? If someone compliments your shoes, and you respond with "Oh, I got them on sale at Payless" instead of saying "Thank you!" you discount the message that person was attempting to convey. A compliment is an example of a validation. It's a token of someone's appreciation for the value they perceive you possess. It doesn't matter if someone compliments your clothing, your hairstyle, or an aspect of your character. When you receive a compliment, it is your opportunity to make an energetic connection with the person complimenting you. Begin to say "Thank you, I am receiving" and watch the other person's eyes light up and see the joy it brings them.

When you can't receive a compliment without discounting it, you are actually robbing the other person of an opportunity to connect with you.

How do you feel about receiving money in your enterprise? Do you feel validated and reaffirmed that others see value in your product, service, or opportunity, or do you feel guilty for taking other people's money? Do you feel good about your clients investing in improving the quality of their lives through your enterprise, or do you worry about disappointing them? It is important that you become conscious of how you feel about receiving money. If you are still subconsciously operating from a position of "Don't take money from strangers" and feel guilty about business transactions with friends, relatives, and people in your circle of influence, you will find very quickly that there isn't anyone left to market to!

Understand that people buy emotionally when they feel good about the perceived value in the product or service they purchase. People will buy from you because they like you, but they will join you in an entrepreneurial venture when they respect you. To succeed in free enterprise, you require both clients and collaborators in order to create profit. Profit is what is left after the bills are paid and the overhead accounted for. Profit is where your salary should be coming from each month in your enterprise. You should have a bank account for your business that is separate from your personal account. You should also be clear about the amount of money in each account, and where this money is coming from. If 100% of your money is coming from your enterprise, then you want to be in a position to reward yourself with a salary that leaves money in both accounts at the end of each month. If you are finding you have more month left at the end of your money, perhaps it is time to reevaluate your spending habits.

Short-Term Sacrifices for Long-Term Gains

Successful entrepreneurs generally live nonconsumptive lifestyles. They do not spend every penny of profit they achieve in a calendar day, week, month, quarter, or year. If your goal is to create an existence where your options are not limited by money, you will first be required to live within your means. This may mean waiting to make a luxurious purchase for a few years, but when you do, you will be able to do so without it affecting your bank account or going into debt on a credit card. Imagine how rewarding that would be!

As you continue to exchange risk for reward in your enterprise, realize that achieving big dreams requires big actions, and it requires a different level of focus than the average person has. It means being able to put some desires on the shelf temporarily in order to produce results. It means short-term sacrifice for long-term gain, and only you will ever give yourself the permission to make this choice. Success may mean letting go of a few habits that no longer serve you. When I decided to build a career as an entrepreneur, I volunteered to give up television. I replaced the time I previously spent watching sitcoms with personal development and building my business. I chose to reward myself with information such as books like this for inspiration as I began to transform my life.

Did I let go of every pleasurable or extracurricular activity? Absolutely not! As I developed a better dialogue with myself about money and prosperity, and as I improved my habits, I created blocks of time for situations outside of our business that I enjoy. I currently run marathons and am an accomplished equestrian. Both of these pursuits require blocks of time away from our business to enjoy them. I have learned to be more productive and focused during my time in our office so I can permit myself to be away from our enterprise without feeling guilty that I left tasks unfinished. Again, this is a matter of giving myself permission. This is also the permission only you can give yourself to enjoy the life you are creating!

If you wait for other people to give you permission, I can guarantee you are in for a long nap. Have you ever dreamed of becoming a millionaire? Give yourself permission to acknowledge your dreams, to romance how it will feel to profit and prosper.

Notes

_____
_____
_____
_____
_____
_____
_____
_____
_____
_____
_____
_____
_____
_____
_____
_____
_____
_____
_____
_____
_____
_____
_____

Notes

_____

_____

_____

_____

_____

_____

_____

_____

_____

_____

_____

_____

_____

_____

_____

_____

_____

_____

_____

_____

_____

_____

_____

_____

_____

_____

_____

4

THE POWER OF SELF-ESTEEM

Self-acceptance and self-esteem are two very powerful experiences you can begin to create for yourself right now in this moment. Each could be a book in and of itself, and indeed, many books have been written to assist people to improve their self-esteem. I am linking them together in this chapter because I have discovered through my own growth that self-acceptance is the foundation for creating a great self-esteem.

Self-esteem is not to be confused with self-confidence. Self-confidence is how capable you feel in a situation. It is very easy to feel confident about your ability to perform in a job if this is what you have been doing for most of your life. But now here you are, an entrepreneur, and if this is new to you, you may find that your foundation of self-confidence is beginning to wobble if you have not also developed a strong sense of self-esteem.

Self-Esteem and Self-Acceptance

Self-esteem is how you feel about you, and self-acceptance is the ability to approve of every aspect of yourself as a whole, understanding that as a human being you are in a constant process of growth and transition. Consider for a moment your role models for self-esteem. As a child, did you grow up in a family that fostered a great sense of self for each family member? If your family was dysfunctional, you are in great company! Most people have not come from a healthy, functional family, and each and every one of us carries beliefs and doubts about ourselves based on our childhood experiences. Unless at some point in time you were fortunate enough to have people in your life who accepted and felt good about themselves who you could mentor with and model yourself after, it can be very challenging as an adult to create a great self-esteem.

Developing a great self-esteem is critical to success in business as an entrepreneur. After all, if you do not feel good about yourself, it is very challenging to market your uniqueness and value if you are not able to recognize it. Recognizing your value begins with accepting yourself fully exactly as you are today. It is so easy to get caught up in the idea of "When _____ changes, I will feel good about myself." The paradox is that until you accept where you are in life physically and where you are in your internal growth emotionally, even when you achieve what you desire you will still feel the same way about yourself. Self-acceptance does not mean that you stagnate in your personal or business growth. It means that you begin to view your progress and current situation more objectively (without judgment), realizing that no matter how much you grow, you will always have areas where you seek development. This is why success is a process, not a destination, and the key to this game is to feel good about where you are and who you are becoming on your journey.

Your Internal Critic

Your emotions play a huge role in your ability to accept yourself. Remember, your emotions attached to the events you experience are what give your beliefs about yourself and the world around you their power. Inside each and every one of us lives an internal critic as well as a voice of understanding and reason. Your critic is the voice that tells you, "You are not good enough, not intelligent enough, unlikely to succeed, unattractive, unlovable," and a multitude of other messages. This is the voice that tells you the same traits and character flaws you are willing to look beyond in other people are the predominating aspects of your character and are unforgivable when you look at yourself. This is the voice that creates anger, embarrassment, guilt, and shame when you reflect on how you operate in life. This voice bases your value as a human being on what you do, not on who you are. When the self-deprecating messages from your internal critic receive more attention than the approving messages in your continuous stream of internal dialogue, this is when you begin to feel guilty and disgusted about your behavior. When you turn all of your attention to listen to your critical voice and believe its message is the absolute truth, it becomes easy to be swept away by a deluge of disapproval, reproach, disparagement, and blame.

Your Voice of Reason

On the other side of this internal equation, you also have a voice of understanding and reason. Becoming conscious and paying more attention to this voice will affect not only how you feel about yourself, but also everything you say, do, and think. The way you feel about yourself affects the way you view the world. When you feel good about your performance in life, life becomes more rewarding and satisfying, and the situations you desire seem to magically fall into place. The messages you receive from your voice of understanding and reason tell you, "You are lovable, you are good, you are worthy, you are learning and growing, you are beautiful in spirit, and you can learn the skills to create success." This is the voice that affirms the good in you in every situation, even when you react poorly to the present moment. It is by definition objective, and constantly validates your worth as a human being; unlike the critic, this voice does not judge your intrinsic value by your actions. This is the voice of self-acceptance that we are all born with and then learn to doubt through interactions with our parents, classmates, teachers and society as we become adults.

Creating Realistic Expectations

One of the predominant issues I assist my clients with is self-acceptance. If you have been reading this chapter nodding your head at the internal critic and then realizing that you do not spend much time with your voice of reason, then it is no wonder you have had some challenges along the way. Once again, you are in good company! The key to creating self-acceptance is to begin to create realistic expectations about yourself and the world around you. This means creating realistic goals and scenarios which are achievable as you continue the process of growth and development. It means developing new habits of thought and emotion regarding what you experience through repetition and exposure now that you are becoming conscious of how your beliefs are created. To accept yourself, you must begin releasing your habits, your patterns of judgment, and your negative self-talk. Realize that this will be a process, not an instantaneous transformation.

Learning a language of love and acceptance is akin to learning a foreign language for most of us. Consider for a moment how much time you have had to practice you skills of criticism and negative self-talk. Be willing to give yourself at least one tenth of that time to begin to change and create some proficiency in your new language. If you began taking a Spanish class tomorrow and your native language was English, you would require time and practice to become fluent in this new language. Even after years of study, you might find yourself at a loss for the right word now and then, and you might even find yourself slipping back into English when your intention was to speak in Spanish. Understand that, just like learning a foreign language, you may forget words at times and catch yourself listening to your internal critic. What is important is that you begin to neutralize and release this critic from your consciousness through repetition and experience over time, without placing an unrealistic expectation on yourself to do so perfectly.

It is also important to understand that, as a human being, you are entitled to experience the full realm of human emotion. In fact, I believe it is our responsibility—defined as "the ability to respond"—to learn how to experience, observe, and release every emotion on the scale, from love to hate and from anger to joy. If you have created two categories of emotions in your belief system, they are probably labeled "Good/Right" and Bad/Wrong" and look something like this:

Good/Right	Bad/Wrong
Love	Hate
Joy	Anger
Happiness	Sadness
Honor	Shame
Innocence	Guilt
Inspired	Hopeless

Good/Right	Bad/Wrong
Capable	Inadequate
Valuable	Useless
Victorious	Defeated
Intelligent	Stupid
Desirable	Unattractive
Exciting	Boring

What if you removed the labels from your emotions and just accepted them for how you feel with no judgment? Emotions are not good or bad, right or wrong. They simply ARE. The way you choose to express your emotions might lead to desirable or undesirable responses and situations, but emotions themselves do not have these moral characteristics.

As Simple as Breathing

Experiencing emotions can be as simple as breathing. If you were to ask me, "Erica, how do I exhale?" I would respond by asking, "Why are you holding your breath?" Exhaling is the normal sequence following an inhalation. Exhaling is normal; preventing an exhalation requires effort. The same is true when you hold onto your emotions. I have assisted clients who suppressed their positive feelings as well as those who suppressed their negative emotions. Those who suppressed their joy and happiness often found that the volume of their expression of these feelings was simply too loud for the people around them, and they responded by muting them within their bodies. Life becomes a new world of laughter and ease when they allow these feelings to surface.

Many people have challenges with releasing emotions such as anger, guilt, and shame. These are the emotions that cause illness and disease within your body if left to fester long enough. Your body only has so much energy with which to operate, and when you expend tremendous amounts of energy repressing your emotions, your body compensates by using energy that would otherwise be used to create healing or ensure the proper function of your organ and your glands. Our bodies are amazing in their capacity to heal themselves and are constantly seeking a condition called "homeostasis." In homeostasis, your body is able to heal itself instantly whenever it's bombarded by an illness, virus, or external toxin of any kind. Because your energy is in perfect harmony within you, a breakdown is just not possible. If this sounds amazing to you, now consider this: your body can only operate as efficiently as your mind allows. When your focus is on suppressing your anger because you believe anger is not okay, your entire body goes into resistance. Medical studies have shown that in this state, the cells in your body actually become smaller. Your entire physiological and spiritual being contracts to keep that one emotion in check. What a waste of precious energy! This is the same situation that leaves you feeling emotionally exhausted and drained at the end of the day.

Good news! This entire reflex can be neutralized with one simple concept: exhale! Release the emotion as you do a breath! You can do this by breathing deeply, filling your entire torso with air, then releasing the breath and repeating this several times. This is particularly effective when you are in an environment not conducive to raging or screaming. When you are alone, you can create a physical release for these emotions. You can throw an unadulterated temper tantrum in the privacy of your own home, and no one will see you or even know about it. The rage police are not going to take due note of your lack of composure and call your family, friends, and collaborators to let them know you lost it. You can punch pillows, scream, and fling yourself onto a bed—whatever creates a release of emotion. If you are worried someone might hear you, simply get a pillow, hold it with both hands, bring it up to your face and scream into it! This is where you can give yourself permission to say all of those ugly thoughts you have been repressing, because if no one else ever hears them, they cannot hurt anyone.

Emotional Release

You may be wondering, what on earth does all of this have with success as an entrepreneur? My answer is unequivocally: everything! To succeed in this game requires emotional resilience, which means it is not easy to rattle your cage. You will experience challenges and triumphs. You will come across people in your business that remind you of people from your past, and you do not want your emotional past creating your entrepreneurial future. When your emotions have been suppressed, they boil under the surface of your consciousness like water in a teakettle, and all it takes is one more match under the kettle to make it scream.

Emotional release has been one of my greatest challenges and is also one of my greatest triumphs as I continue my journey. Emotional release cannot only lengthen your fuse, it can keep the candle from burning at both ends. I have been in both places emotionally; I've been in a place where my fuse was so short, people did not want to converse with me, and I've also been in the position where my emotions were burning one end of the candle while my efforts to suppress them as I dealt with them were burning the other end. Let me tell you, there is not much room in the middle in this situation. My emotional pressure shows up in my body, and there are days when I wake up looking like I gained twenty-five pounds overnight! Of course I haven't, but this is my body's way of letting me know it's time to acknowledge what is going on inside me emotionally. Some people suffer headaches or spinal subluxation. I am learning to release my physiological inconsistency. All this requires is a few moments to ask, "What is this really about? What I am I feeling and why?" When the reason for the pressure becomes apparent, and I allow myself to release whatever expectation I was creating about my performance in the future, my body releases as well. A lot of what I am learning is to become a victor, not a victim of my physical circumstance. Being bloated isn't fun, but if I constantly worry about being bloated, I too, will receive exactly what I expect.

You will find in your journey that situations as a business owner can escalate and feel overwhelming very quickly. It is never the situation itself, but the emotions connected to it and the belief created as a result which overwhelms you. Remember that you are the creator of your emotional reality. You can choose your emotional response to any given situation. This is emotional resilience. Most people feel small in relation to their emotions, but remember you are the creator here. By default, this means there is never an emotion you will ever feel that is larger or more powerful than you are. There is never a situation you can't neutralize, and there is never a goal you will ever seek that you cannot achieve when you accept and honor the powerful, unique individual that you are.

Notes

_____
_____
_____
_____
_____
_____
_____
_____
_____
_____
_____
_____
_____
_____
_____
_____
_____
_____
_____
_____
_____
_____

Notes

_____

_____

_____

_____

_____

_____

_____

_____

_____

_____

_____

_____

_____

_____

_____

_____

_____

_____

5

THE POWER OF POSTURE

Posture is another key ingredient in creating entrepreneurial success. By posture, I'm not talking about how erect your spine is or balancing a stack of books on your head as you walk around your home. The information I have to share with you about posture relates to your conscious mental projections and how you resonate in life. You see, your posture is really your presence. It's how you project your energy, and the people you do business with will connect to the energy you emit.

If you are constantly rehashing your past experiences, challenges, failures, triumphs, victories, or defeats, how much of your energy can you tap into in the present moment? If you are so anxious about what the future might hold for you, how much energy do you have left to create connections in the present? The answer is that you won't have as much energy as you require to create the connections and collaborations that will produce results in your enterprise. Attracting quality people to your business as clients or collaborators will require you to focus much more of your energy in the present moment. When your energy is present, YOU are present. This means you resonate from an entirely different frequency than the masses of society in order to collaborate with the classes.

We live in a universe where energy is neither created nor destroyed; it is only transformed. Every thought, every emotion, every particle of matter, every atom of your body is made of energy. Imagine what you could create if you allowed yourself to tap into that energy! Energy vibrates on different frequencies. For instance, a sound wave carries a different energy than a light wave, and a positive emotion carries a different energy than a negative one. If you seek to attract positive, motivated people to your business, then you must learn to emit the energy that will resonate with those people. When this happens, the people you seek will be drawn to you like magnets. This is because energy attracts energy that is vibrating at the same rate.

Your posture—how you project your energy—has a direct impact on the people and the world around you. Every experience you have each and every day is a product of your expectation. That's how powerful you are! Your mind has the ability to send your expectations out to the Universe, and the Universe complies by providing you with situations to affirm those projections. This can be a tough pill to swallow at first, because it means accepting complete responsibility for the life you are currently experiencing. Remember, responsibility means *the ability to respond*. If you desire to change the people and situations you attract, the key is changing your posture.

The Seven Types of Posture

I see people operating from seven key types of posture each and every day. It is essential that you begin to understand where people are operating from so that you can connect and collaborate with them without being affected by their posture in that moment. This means knowing how to neutralize someone's anger so that you do not subconsciously assist them to create another situation to remain angry. It also means neutralizing your emotions at times in order to capitalize on the posture of someone who is peaceful and calm. Your posture can absolutely either enhance your connections with others or sabotage them.

Over-Posturing – Too Angry to Connect
Over-posturing occurs when someone is too angry and aggressive to connect with other people. This type of person is constantly arguing and validating their position before it has ever been challenged. Over-posturing creates a tremendous amount of emotional and energetic distance between yourself and others, subconsciously driving away the very people you are

seeking to connect with. People who operate from this type of posture often harbor a belief that they are not lovable or not good enough. They may feel that they were never listened to as children, so as adults, they perceive that in order to have their ideas, thoughts, and emotions heard, they must express them aggressively or else be ignored. Others perceive this posture as loud, rude, annoying, and argumentative. It can also be very intimidating if you are on the receiving end of this type of energy.

If you find yourself operating this way from time to time, it is important to recognize that you are actually sabotaging the opportunity to connect and collaborate with someone who could enhance your current experience. If you find yourself on the receiving end of this energy, realize that you are receiving the emotions of a hurt and angry child channeled through an adult body and mind; it's really not a personal attack on you.

Neutralizing this type of posture can seem intimidating. Let's face it, none of us enjoys spending time being angry or feeling the force of someone else's anger even when we understand it and are not taking it personally. It is important to determine exactly where your boundaries are—when enough is enough and when such a person no longer qualifies for your time if he or she continues to operate this way. Sometimes neutralizing this type of posture can only happen after one or both parties take some time and space to calm down. If you are the receiver in this situation, remember that the person operating from this posture probably has no idea how angry or aggressive they sound to you. If you respond in anger by becoming offended or defensive, your energy becomes combative as well. Now, instead of being in a situation with an antagonist and a protagonist, you will find yourself in a situation with two antagonists butting heads with absolutely no hope of collaboration.

You can always use questions in order to create space to determine if there is any neutral ground to collaborate on. You can say, "I can appreciate your position. What are you angry about?" A statement followed by a question works because it not only validates the other person's emotions, it also lets them know you are interested in *why* they are so aggressive or angry. I have used this tool thousands of times, and provided I am asking the question from my peace, I am able to disarm an over-posturer in a matter of seconds. Remember, this is someone who does not feel heard, justified, or validated. Validating that you are indeed receiving their message loud and clear is a first step toward creating neutral ground to continue a conversation; just be sure to use this tool *before* you allow yourself to become offended by this person's attitude. If you wait until you are already offended and feeling angry and violated, your reaction will fuel the fire rather than extinguish it. This is why knowing your own emotional boundary is so important.

If you know that you yourself operate from this posture in certain situations, begin asking yourself, *What am I angry about? Who never listened to me? Whose attention have I been subconsciously seeking in life that I never received as a child?* These unresolved emotions connected to past experiences will continue to influence your adult relationships and business interactions as long as they remain unresolved. What happens is that we attract people into our lives to reaffirm the beliefs we've created as a result of a past event or experience. When you feel the urge to validate, justify or defend yourself, take a deep breath and give yourself a moment to relax and feel safe. Realize that there is nothing personal in business, and the only person you are ever going to be required to be good enough for in business is *you*. There is really very little judgment from others in the entrepreneurial arena. It's the critical judge within us who creates many of our conflicts and confrontations.

Why is it even important to understand and neutralize an over-posturer? It seems as if this is the type of person you would absolutely want to blow off and release from your life. The reason is that many obsessive, compulsive, productive type-A personalities with unresolved anger issues operate this way unconsciously every day. These are also the driven doers of society, the movers, the shakers, the rebels, and the renegades—the very people who will produce from pride when the chips are down and the deck seems stacked against them. These people can produce the most results for you in your business, so if you can learn to communicate with and neutralize this type of person's energy, you can also capitalize on their strengths and abilities. You'll create the connection in this instance, but once it's established it often lasts for a lifetime because of the respect you create by confronting and disarming this person from your peace.

Under-Posturing – Too Meek to Be Heard

Under-posturing is the exact opposite of over-posturing. This is typically the posture of the great caretakers in society. Their message is, *Can't we all just get along?* There is nothing wrong with being amiable, but success in the free market requires you to project your energy with enough power for your message to be heard and felt by the people you are seeking to connect with. When other people sense that your posture is meek or submissive, they lose respect for you and your message. They may like you, but they will also naturally challenge you. They may become your friend, yet not buy from you.

I've assisted many of my clients with this amiable personality type to release their anxiety about what might happen in a confrontation with someone who challenges them. A-type personalities will cut to the chase and ask you questions like "What's this all about?" in the first thirty to sixty seconds of a conversation, especially when they sense you are someone they can challenge. I have found that most people who dread confrontation in any form do so because they have had negative experiences in confrontational situations. However, it is possible to confront someone in business without creating conflict. This is a skill developed over time through repetition and experience. If you feel people are pushing you around in business and in life, then it's time to create strength in your projection and begin demanding that your message be heard and acknowledged!

If you are too meek, begin to strengthen your posture by determining exactly where the lines are that you will not allow anyone to cross. This applies to personal relationships as well as business transactions. It can be easy to suddenly find yourself in a compromising situation if you feel guilty saying no or anxious about voicing an opinion that may conflict with someone else's. By knowing exactly what you will or won't do and what you will or won't settle for, you begin to create a new awareness of where these boundaries lie. By upholding them for your own personal integrity, you will begin creating the required strength in your personal foundation in order to begin adding some power to your posture.

A great exercise is to scream into a pillow. Many people are too meek in their message because they are actually very angry inside and are worried that if they ever released any of this anger, they would explode and would never be able to stop. I've written more about this in Chapter Seven, The Power of Forgiveness. Screaming into a pillow provides you with a very safe and effective way to release some of the emotions you fear letting go of. It's safe because no one around you will hear you or be affected by your emotions. It's liberating to simply say what you feel, and you will be relieved to finally let go.

When you let go of whatever has been keeping you meek and playing small, you will be amazed at how much more effective your time and actions will become in your business.

Powerful Posture

Free enterprise is a competitive marketplace. There will always be someone at the top (Mark Victor Hansen, for example), and there will always be a new star on the rise. If you are the rising star on your way to the top, you want to be sure you have every advantage, and developing some power in your posture will greatly assist your ascent.

This does *not* mean becoming rude, aggressive, or abrasive in your interactions with other people. I have personally met Mark Victor Hansen on numerous occasions, and he is one of the kindest, most philanthropic men I have ever met, with an absolutely genuine love of people. Yet he exudes an energy that commands respect from those around him. When he speaks, others listen. This is the kind of energy you want to develop as you continue your journey.

Remember that my definition of power is *emotional autonomy*. If you give yourself permission to be yourself, regardless of the circumstances, you have the ability to transform the energy in a room, or in a phone conversation. The following is a great example of how staying in your power and in your energy can enhance your results.

One evening after a live conference call, a woman from New York emailed us a question about purchasing the special package Jeff had offered on the call. She sent me the email at 11:55 PM her time, and I returned her message with a phone call within ten minutes. When I called her, she asked me pseudo-aggressively if I was aware of the time in New York. I replied, "Absolutely, but I can tell from your stereo in the background that your party just got started." She stopped, laughed, and said, "That was good, girlfriend; let me go get my credit card!" In that moment, a potentially antagonistic [or adversarial] situation was neutralized and became favorable for both of us.

It would have been easy for me to have become rattled and have ended the conversation with this woman when she challenged me. Instead, I stayed in my power and found a creative way to neutralize her objection to the time of night I called her by letting her know I knew there was no way she was on her way to bed with the dance music she had blaring in the background. Her response happened to be very positive, but if it had been less than desirable, this would have informed me about the potential this woman and I had for collaborating. I have also had people request that I return their call the following day, which I have gladly done.

Developing a powerful posture begins with feeling good about yourself and your message. Once again, this is called self-esteem. When you feel good about your posture and your product or service, you will begin taking situations like these much less personally and will move into a position where you constantly seek room for collaboration rather than disconnection.

I have been involved in sales and marketing since 1996, and believe me, my posture then was much different than it is now, and my results reflected it. I have experienced the transition from a panicked posture of "How soon can I hang up and get out of this uncomfortable situation?" to the powerful posture of being able to neutralize a conversation to determine where there is room for collaboration. This transition happened through growth, development, repetition, and experience.

You have the opportunity to be an actor or actress in every conversation you have on the phone. If you do not feel powerful yet, act as if you already are! No one else will ever know the difference unless you tell them you are uncomfortable. Give yourself the power to say what you feel instead of reaching for the perfect response. This will allow you

63

to be much more genuine, and it is this integrity of character that people will buy.

Passionate Posture

What are you passionate about in life? What motivates you? What gets you excited and brings light to your eyes? This is not about getting hyped, jazzed, or pumped up, but people respond positively when they hear passion in your voice and feel passion in your energy. What is your entrepreneurial purpose, also known as your why? Staying connected to your passion, the reason you became an entrepreneur in the first place, will greatly assist your posture in the face of adversity on your journey.

When you are able to tap into your passion and resonate from this posture when challenges arise, you give yourself the power to immediately impact the potential outcome of the situation. Remember, energy projected attracts like energy back to it. It can be far too easy in this game to feel overwhelmed by adversity and give in to negative or self-deprecating criticism. Reconnecting to your passion during these times allows you to look beyond your current crisis to your long-term gain or objective.

It's the challenges you triumph over and the lessons you learn through your decisions that build character on your journey to success. I have yet to meet a successful person who hasn't bounced through a few chuckholes on the road to financial freedom. Perception is reality; your passion will be felt by others and they will be influenced by it.

I have a conference call series I host twice a year called "The Psychology of Releasing Weight." I began this forum when I realized that my emotions were holding my physical weight in place, not my diet or exercise habits. At one point in my life, I was exercising at my health club three to four hours a day with no results! I was living the definition of insanity by repeating the same physical actions over and over while expecting a different result. It wasn't until I changed my emotional dialogue with myself that my body ever had enough space to release. I'm sharing this with you because I remained passionate about my exercise routine and experience even while I was frustrated and looking for answers. The other members of my club could feel my passion for creating health in my body, and would let me know how much they enjoyed my presence in our group exercise classes, or down in the weight room. They said it inspired them to stay focused and motivated and committed to their own routines.

My point here is that success is a continual process, and there is always room for more growth and for more results. Staying connected to your reason for being in the process will not only see you through any challenges you experience on your way, but will also inspire those around you to travel on the journey with you. What a great support system! This is not about being positive, it's about feeling passionate. Passion will fuel your engine when you feel the train beginning to stall. Passion will create the momentum to carry you through growth to stability. When you project your passion through your energy, people around you will want to stay connected with you and will want to be a part of the business and experience you are creating.

Collaborative Posture vs. Competitive Posture

Collaborative vs. competitive—This may sound like semantics at first, but as an entrepreneur I have found that there is never any competition in true collaboration. I have had many opportunities to create what I believed would be a collaboration and then found myself in a competitive situation. I have also had many opportunities to collaborate and build relationships with people who could easily be perceived as direct competition.

Collaboration happens when the end result leaves all contributors feeling fulfilled and satisfied. Each person doesn't necessarily receive the same result because of the collaboration, but everyone benefits and feels good about the outcome. True collaboration is what creates the difference between building a business that has "flash in the pan" results and one that prospers and grows for the long run.

By default, competition will always exist in the marketplace. As you continue your entrepreneurial journey, collaboration will not only separate you, the cream, from the milk, but will also allow you to build relationships with other entrepreneurs as you grow together. At times this may mean extending yourself for someone else to use as leverage as they grow and build their business. When you are able to do this in absolute faith that the other person will do likewise when they are able, you put yourself in a collaborative situation.

Competition occurs when one participant begins to perceive the objective as scarce and in short supply and actively demands more of it than the other. This objective can be money, opportunity, great people, connections, relationships, etc. Regardless of the resource being pursued, competition is created when one person becomes threatened that there may not be enough for both participants and begins to undermine the collaboration to receive more of the spoils immediately. In competition there is always a winner and a loser, and often competition sabotages relationships, creating enough discord to inhibit future ventures.

When you project a collaborative posture, you look at the long-term vision. You move into the situation willing to sacrifice short-term results for long-term gain. You focus more on building rapport within the relationship than you do the immediate outcome of the venture because you are focused on attracting like-minded people whose energy and goals align with yours. When this happens, you receive the opportunity to collect on the synergy of your efforts not only in the present, but also as you both continue to grow and develop. This can happen with individuals in different industries as well as those in your industry. Once again, this is about energy and projecting what you seek to attract. The more collaborative your attitude and posture becomes, the more collaborative people and situations you will attract.

Peaceful Posture

Peace is the key to resonating powerfully, passionately, and collaboratively. When you create peace in your own emotional dialogue, the tranquility within you will begin to manifest around you. Peace and chaos cannot exist in the same instant, and peace will neutralize and dissipate chaos in an instant. When you project your energy from your peace, you will find you are able to neutralize anger effortlessly, and any confrontations will not create conflict. You will find a different level of harmony in your relationships and conversations. This is when you can seek eye contact from another person and they meet your gaze willingly, feeling something positive is waiting for them in their experience with you.

Peaceful posture allows you to flow with life instead of creating resistance. It is the key to combining the three most powerful postures to create one ultimate frequency of energy to attract abundance. This is where you can hear the meaning behind the words people use and to respond intuitively to the emotional message you feel, not just the words you hear. When you are in your peace, you are able to respond to the situations you experience instead of react, and typically overreact, to them.

Developing an Empowering Posture

Each and every one of us currently operates or has operated from all of these different postures. There is no perfect posture to resonate from 100 percent of the time. Life will test you, and you will attract both positive situations to reinforce your development as well as challenges to test you. Decide where you desire to improve how you resonate and focus on developing the emotional foundation and skills to allow you to spend more time in that energy. You may have to have some experiences to teach you the lesson required to complete your shift in consciousness.

For instance, I have learned in situations where I'm feeling attacked or invalidated to stop and say, "I deserve better." If I feel I am not receiving the respect I deserve, there are instances where I actually make this statement out loud. Other times, I'll just say it silently in my own mind with the intention of creating the resolution I DO DESERVE. I have found that this is a very profound and noninflammatory way to draw a boundary about what I will and will not allow myself to experience. It is also a very powerful sentence that commands instant respect that I state from my peace to create what I desire instead of settling for what just happens.

If you begin to resonate from a posture that empowers you sixty to seventy-five percent of the time, I guarantee your results will begin to shift in your favor. Remember, perfection is not possible... this is about consistently choosing your reality to create exceptional results.

Notes

_____

_____

_____

_____

_____

_____

_____

_____

_____

_____

_____

_____

_____

_____

_____

_____

_____

_____

_____

_____

_____

Notes

_____

_____

_____

_____

_____

_____

_____

_____

_____

_____

_____

_____

_____

_____

_____

_____

_____

_____

_____

_____

6

THE POWER OF LANGUAGE

As an entrepreneur, it is very important that you begin to study language and understand its importance in creating results. Language tells you a lot about the person speaking when you begin to pay attention to the messages behind someone's words. Your language is a projection of your thoughts, feelings, and emotions. Your words then lead to actions, which in turn create results. If you are seeking big results as an entrepreneur, it is imperative that you begin speaking an empowering language of success to assist you in accomplishing your objectives.

A Powerful Tool

Most people give little or no thought to the words they use in everyday life. In my opinion, it is not a coincidence that most people who do not pay attention to their words are also willing to settle for average results rather than pursue exceptional outcomes. When was the last time you gave any thought to the language you use? Language is a powerful tool you can use to serve you on your journey. If your language has developed from a position of lack and scarcity, then the words you use will attract more struggle to you to perpetuate the reality you believe you are living in. If your language has developed from a position of prosperity and abundance, the words you use will attract situations and opportunities to you to validate this belief as well.

As I have stated, in our universe, energy cannot be created or destroyed; it can only be transformed. The words you use are a transformation of the energy of the thoughts, feelings, and emotions that you are expressing. The energy you project will be the energy you attract, and your results will manifest accordingly. This is why it is so important that you become conscious of the words you use if success is what you seek. I have realized on my own journey that successful entrepreneurs and successful businesspeople use a different vocabulary than those who struggle or barely get by. I have had the opportunity to spend time with many self-made millionaires, and they all share a common respect for the spoken word. They all are extremely aware of the words they choose to speak.

Do You "Need" or Do You "Deserve"?

Your words either empower you or disempower you. Empowering words express a decision and a commitment, while disempowering words reveal hesitation, lack of focus, and inaction. If you ask me what one word you could release from your vocabulary to change your results, my answer would be the word "need." One definition of the word need is "a lack of something requisite, desirable, or useful." When you say, "I need to make more money," all you are speaking is the reality that you do not have enough money and that you are experiencing a lack of financial support. The word need has a very low level of energy, because by definition, a need expresses lack, meaning the situation can never be fulfilled. This energy then attracts situations and experiences to you to perpetuate your need so you can receive what you expect by never having enough.

Perhaps you find a new business partner or collaborator to partner with whose influence is going to open an influential network for you to create results with. You see how this one connection will bring you thousands of dollars, and then within a day or two you experience an emergency or some other major catastrophe which will require all of your expected revenue to fix. This situation continues to justify and validate your need for more money. Even though you were anticipating a great windfall, your spoke your need into existence and thus attracted a situation to perpetuate your lack of money. It does not matter how much money you are able to achieve if you are never able to retain any of it! As long as you perceive you need more, whether it is more money, more love, more opportunity, more recognition, etc., you will also consistently attract situations to you to negate what you receive to edify your original words and emotional position of what you need.

If you will simply replace the word "need" with the word "deserve," and develop the habit of saying "I deserve," you will notice that your results change. The word deserve can be defined as "to be worthy of" and once again, has a Latin root meaning "to serve." Deserve means to feel worthy to receive whatever it is you desire to attract. The statement "I deserve to receive more money" will create an entirely different experience than saying "I need more money." "I deserve more money" sends a message that I am worthy of receiving money to serve me in my purpose, thus I have no resistance separating me from the money I seek.

Do you feel how different this message is? Rather than projecting that you have a need, meaning a lack that by definition will perpetuate without ever finding fulfillment, you project, "I am worthy to receive exactly what I require to serve my purpose, and no resistance will separate me from it." If your purpose is to purchase a new car, you will attract the money to do so without also attracting a situation to divert the money you were going to use to purchase your new car to address a different issue. Instead, you will now attract the money you feel you are worthy to receive as defined by the word deserve so that you can use the money for its intended purpose.

Spoken Words Create Expectancy

In her book, *The Game of Life and How to Play It*, Florence Scovel Shinn writes, "A person, knowing the power of the word, becomes very careful of his conversation. He has only to watch the reaction of his words to know that they do 'not return void.' Through his spoken word, man is continually making laws for himself." What she means is that your spoken word creates expectancy in your subconscious mind, thus attracting the situation or experience required to validate your expectancy.

If you are having challenges digesting this concept, consider the psychology of superstitions. Carrying a rabbit's foot or a horseshoe will not bring you lucky situations in and of themselves. It is your emotional connection to the belief that these are good luck charms that create your expectancy of good fortune. This is also why Mondays are often challenging, while Fridays are easy. It is your subconscious expectation that attracts people, situations, and experiences to validate your current beliefs.

Replace Resistance Words

I will assist you with identifying and replacing some of the most commonly used words that create resistance with words that will allow you to transition to nonresistance. There is a common misconception in our society that is must be difficult, draining, and time-consuming to produce the results which will enhance our lives and experiences. In reality, we receive what we subconsciously expect and speak into existence. If you have ever heard yourself say, "The only way to do anything right is to do it yourself," then it is very probable that when you assign someone else to a task, you receive a result from that person which is substandard to your expectation of a job well done. The irony is that you set yourself up to receive this exact situation through your previous statement. This situation can be neutralized instantly by replacing the disempowering statement with an empowering one, such as "I effortlessly communicate exactly what I expect so that when I assign a task to someone else they complete it exactly as if I performed the task myself." Do you see how much easier your life can become just by changing a few simple words?

Words of Resistance	Words of Ease
Try	Will
Need	Deserve
Work	Produce
Hard	Easy
Maybe	Yes or No
Think	Feel
Yeah, Uh-huh	Yes

Words of Resistance	Words of Ease
Nah, Nope	No
Cost	Value
Busy	Productive
Struggle	Effortless
Help	Assist

All of the above words of ease are words for you to consider incorporating into your vocabulary. These are words of prosperity and abundance—emotional as well as monetary. Here are a few statements I use in my life which have positively impacted my results:

New Empowering Statement	Statement to Release
I deserve to receive exactly what I desire!	I need _____.
I am a productive entrepreneur!	I am so busy!
What is the value?	How much does this cost?
I produce results effortlessly!	I work really hard.
I require/seek assistance.	I need help.
I will.	I'll try.
How do you feel about this information/situation?	What do you think?

Words of resistance usually carry little or no commitment. For instance, if I asked you to try to stand up, you would have challenges performing this task. This is because you will either sit or stand. To say you will try something means you will contemplate it, but eventually take no action. When you ask someone if they will review information about your product or service and they respond with "I'll try," this is a clue as to what they are already telling you they are not going to do.

To succeed as an entrepreneur, you will be required (not you will need) to learn how to provoke other people to take action. Once again, most people are not aware of the words they use or how these words impact their reality. As you become more conscious of your own language, you will also become more aware of the words other people use. You will begin to hear the underlying subconscious messages behind the statements they make. For instance, if someone says to you, "This sounds good, but

75

how much does it cost?" you will receive an insight into their dialogue with money that they had no idea they were broadcasting. I learned very quickly when I worked in industrial diesel engine and generator sales that the price had absolutely nothing to do with the purchase. Until your client or customer understands the value of what you are marketing and understands how it will enhance their life, the sticker price assigned to it is meaningless. Until the value is ascertained, there is no incentive to buy.

In the previous example, you also are receiving a contradictory statement. If your opportunity or product sounds so good, where is the resistance coming from? When you begin to understand why we choose the words we speak, you will begin to communicate on a different emotional level. You will understand that price is never the issue; it is always about perceived value. If you are receiving objections about the price of your product or service, then you might consider changing the way you are presenting the value of what you are marketing.

Communicate Value

Prosperous people do not focus on what a product or service costs; rather they focus on the value that product or service will bring. This is a very important distinction to understand, because when someone asks you the cost of your product or service within the first thirty to sixty seconds of conversation, this should give you a clue about this person's dialogue with money and prosperity. It is always easier to complete business transactions with emotionally, spiritually, or financially prosperous people because they already have the means to complete the transaction. What happens so often is that we feel intimidated by what we perceive we lack in comparison to these people and so resist approaching them with our product or service.

Prosperous people seek ways to add value to their experience, regardless of who presents the opportunity to them. If you speak words of ease and prosperity, you will capture their attention very quickly and they will be much more likely to buy from you. Your language will create a connection to bridge the gap between you. If you speak words of prosperity, you will begin to make deposits in your emotional and spiritual bank account and these deposits will eventually manifest in your physical bank account. How quickly this happens is entirely up to you. The thoughts you think influence the words you speak, which determine the results you receive!

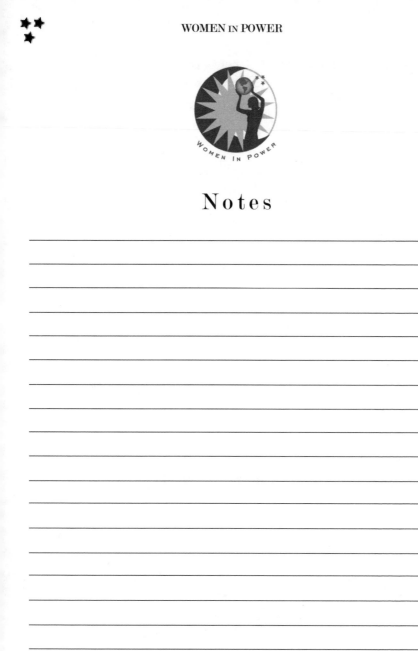

Notes

Notes

_____

_____

_____

_____

_____

_____

_____

_____

_____

_____

_____

_____

_____

_____

_____

_____

_____

_____

_____

_____

WOMEN IN POWER

7

THE POWER OF FORGIVENESS

Forgiveness is a very powerful emotional tool that will greatly assist you as an entrepreneur. People are not perfect. I am not perfect, and neither are you. We are all here doing to best we can each day, both in our personal relationships as well as in our business transactions. Because of our emotional imperfections, conflicts, misunderstandings, miscommunications, and unintended transgressions are common in our interactions with people. Forgiveness is about letting go of the negative emotional connections to these situations, people, and events so we can release our pain and experience more pleasure on our journey.

When you insist on perfection from yourself, it is easy to feel like a constant failure. When you demand perfection from others and from your relationships, you doom these situations from the very beginning. Forgiveness is about releasing the judgment connected to your own imperfections, as well as those of others to create more room for understanding and to restore the connection within yourself, as well as the world around you.

Forgiveness is important because as an entrepreneur you will come across disbelievers, dream stealers, and critics as you journey through free enterprise. It is natural to feel moments of self-doubt and discouragement when receiving input from other people who do not have the same vision as you. Forgiveness allows you to release any bitterness or rancor connected to this information, and it neutralizes the human tendency to redirect the feedback of others as self-criticism. Forgiveness allows you to reclaim your power, whether you are forgiving yourself, another person, or a past experience. Until you release the emotions connected to the events in your life, you will continue to carry them with you into every new encounter. This is why so many people perceive it as rejection when someone else cannot see the value of their idea or business opportunity. Forgiveness creates the path to objectivity, and objectivity allows you to understand another's position instead of assuming there is something lacking in you because they do not see the same value in your product, service, or opportunity as you do.

Many people resist forgiveness because they feel justified in harboring their pain and anger connected to a situation where they felt unjustly treated. They feel that forgiveness would let the other person off the hook. In reality, forgiveness lets you off the hook by creating emotional space in your own internal dialogue. Releasing negative emotions creates space to feel more positive emotions—and your positive emotions are what will enable you to attract the people and situations you desire to your reality.

Seven Misconceptions About Forgiveness

The seven common misconceptions about forgiveness are:

- If I forgive someone, my relationship with that person will immediately improve.

- If I forgive, I will stop feeling anger.

- If I forgive, I relinquish my right to feeling hurt.

- If I forgive, it means that what happened is okay.

- If I forgive, I have to forget.

- If I forgive, I am only required to forgive once.

- Forgiving myself is selfish.

Forgiveness requires courage and the willingness to confront and release your pain. Countless people are willing to harbor resentment and anger, and to continue blaming their past and others for their current circumstances. They are satisfied to remain toxic in their emotions and to contaminate those around them with negativity and dissatisfaction. Practicing the art of forgiveness means deciding that you will not allow the rest of your life to be determined by the unjust and injurious acts of other people, whether they occurred in the past, the present, or may happen again in the future. Forgiveness is one of the keys to creating *emotional autonomy*, my personal definition of power.

As a child, you incorporated into your belief structure the personalities, points of view, mentalities, and belief structures of those closest to you, at least in part. Your self-image was influenced by the approval or disapproval you received from these individuals. Although you were born with a genetic predisposition, every interaction you experience with the people around you, both past and present, impacts your neural wiring. Your brain records your emotional experiences and creates physical neural pathways, paths that connect the electronic impulses released by your neurons to your body. These impulses tell your body how to react physically to the emotions you feel, and in effect, they become the highways that guide you in your relationships. These highways are continually created in your brain as you move through life. This is why it is so easy to create the same situation over and over, or to attract the same kind of relationship over and over. The neural pathways in your brain influence the energy you emit, which acts as a biological attractor, attracting those to you with patterns that in some way correspond to yours.

If your relationships or physical reality are not what you desire, then it is imperative that you understand what input from the past has affected your neural pathways. Until you recognize the emotions connected to the actions you take, you will continue to send a biological signal that attracts people and situations which correspond with the energy you project.

Forgiving the past which led you to your current reality can begin to reprogram your emotions and create new neural pathways in your brain that change your energetic frequency. This allows you to begin attracting people and experiences that resonate with your new frequency, thus creating new empowering experiences and relationships. Forgiveness will allow you to honestly confront the petty grievances and significant wounds from your past that keep you in a state of emotional flight, fight, or freeze when a present situation provokes the emotions from your past to surface. Practicing forgiveness is a way to keep your neural highways up to date so that you can continue your journey to the life you are designing rather than continuing the life you have already experienced. Imagine how much easier it would be to navigate the physical highways in life if new construction and repair could be created instantaneously. Well, your brain has the ability to create new neural pathways in an instant, and when you begin to forgive, to let go, and to release your emotions connected to your past, you begin to create new highways in your brain in that exact same moment.

As I mentioned earlier, no one is perfect, and it is my belief that we all function to the best of our ability each and every day. For me, the ability to forgive my past stems from this belief. If hindsight is 20/20, then doesn't it make sense that you can look at your past from the perspective of the adult that you are today rather than the person you were then? If you were to look at some of the painful memories from the past from this perspective, would it be possible for you to become more objective about them and their significance in your emotional history?

I had the privilege this year of remembering an experience from my early childhood that has affected me my entire life, in both business and personal relationships. As a young child, I suffered from asthma and allergies and even experienced asthma attacks that could have proved fatal. One afternoon when I was about two years old, I had a severe attack, and after it ended I fell asleep. My father was an airline pilot and had to leave that day for a flight. My parents decided not to wake me up to say goodbye before he left, and when I awoke, he was gone. I remember crying inconsolably because I thought he wasn't coming back. I thought because I had been sick and had scared my parents, my father had decided to abandon me. Looking back, I can see my genetic predisposition for control had me internalizing the situation, because if my dad leaving was somehow my fault, then I could change something in me to be good enough to make him come back. In reality, he had just left to do his job, and he would have left and returned a few days later whether I had been sick or not.

The emotions I created connected to this event made me feel that there was something wrong with me, that I was not good enough, that I was bad, and so my dad left. I created my own emotional punishment, and this belief has affected my relationships with men both personally and professionally for much of my life. When I remembered this, I immediately began forgiving myself for my asthma, forgiving my parents for their decision, as well as forgiving the men I had attracted to affirm my beliefs during my life. I began the process of letting go of the negative emotions connected to this and the skewed logic I used as a small child to create them. I finally became aware of the foundation of one of my beliefs and was able to practice the art of forgiveness to begin to let go and change the way I feel about myself in the present.

The Five Stages of Forgiveness:

1. Awareness

Part of what seems so challenging about forgiveness is our fear of reexperiencing our pain. We become anxious when faced with the proposition of excavating past emotions and feeling them again in order to let them go. We resist the idea of feeling as helpless and vulnerable as we did the first time we were wronged.

I am here to tell you firsthand that the anxiety you feel about your emotions is far stronger than the actual emotions themselves. Anxiety is akin to procrastination; it requires far more energy than taking action. You know the pain you carry—it manifests every time a situation or interaction provokes a similar emotion. It is because you have suppressed and carried the pain for so long that it feels overwhelming. Awareness is synonymous with consciousness, and this recognition of how you feel is the first step toward forgiveness.

2. Anger and Sadness

Once you recognize and acknowledge your feelings, anger and sadness are very common emotions. This is because you have been carrying the hurt connected to the situation from your past with you into the present. It is normal to feel angry because of what you experienced, and to feel a sense of loss for what you perceived you missed as well.

Anger can create all kinds of chaos as well as being very cathartic, depending on how you choose to express it. Many artists have created their finest masterpieces from an emotion called angst—channeling their anger through artistic expression. Anger can be a source of immobilization as well as provocation, depending on how you choose to release it. Screaming into a pillow, physical exercise, cleaning, or reorganizing your home can all be very healthy releases for unexpressed anger. Sometimes anger is the very motivator to create results in business as well.

Just remember, you created your anger in the first place. Despite how large it may seem, it will never be bigger than you or overpower you. Give yourself permission to create a strategy for releasing your anger, one that you can repeat to create peace for the rest of your life.

Sadness can feel overwhelming and disorganizing, like you are falling apart. It can create feelings of depression and lethargy. Sadness is often repressed anger, guilt, or blame. Sadness harbored over time will become resentment and will require release. Again, it is normal to feel sad about what was, but also realize that you would not be receiving this information if your experiences had not led you here! Opportunities are never lost; they are seized by the few who are ready. Stop looking at what you didn't get and focus on what you are ready to receive. I guarantee that if you will create this transition of your focus, you will begin to receive the results you desire.

3. Grief

Grief is a part of life. It is normal and healthy to grieve loss, even if the loss you grieve is only a perception of what could have been. People who cannot express grief often erect walls around themselves in an effort to avoid future pain. Unfortunately, these walls also often keep them from feeling deep connections and pleasure as well. How can you possibly connect with other visionaries if you are protecting yourself from sincere and deep relationships to avoid another loss?

Denied grief and anger get displaced onto situations and relationships in the present. This places undue burdens on present-day relationships and subconsciously pushes the very people you seek to connect with away from you.

It is important to feel your pain and to link it to where the wound began in order to create some kind of reason out of the original situation. This will allow you to separate the past from the present so that today does not become a reenactment of yesterday's traumas and struggles. Grief is cleansing—it allows you to feel what is real and reconnect with your personal truth.

4. Acceptance

When you begin acknowledging the experiences that have contributed to your emotional roadmaps, you will gain a new understanding of how the circumstances of your life have impacted you and why. You will begin to understand yourself in a new way. It is very common at this point to want to get rid of all of the negative emotions connected to your past in an effort to never experience them again. As a human being, it is normal to encounter your own self-loathing as you increase your self-understanding. In delving into the feelings surrounding a forgiveness issue, it is almost inevitable to encounter the inability to forgive yourself, even if this means simply being in the wrong place at the wrong time, or perhaps being vulnerable, or being unable to stand up for yourself.

Understanding these emotions and the situations surrounding them opens the door to self-acceptance, which allows you to also accept others more easily. Forgiving and accepting yourself leads to forgiving and accepting others. When you can accept yourself exactly as you are, it will become much easier to accept others just as they are, flaws and all. When you can do this, you will begin to see where other people are operating from in their own realities instead of taking their reactions and responses so personally. This is where you begin to accept that it is really not about you, but is so much more about them. When you understand this, you can release the emotional pressure to be perfect and spend more time just being.

5. Letting Go

Letting go allows you to see life more realistically. It allows you to become much more objective about what you can and cannot expect of yourself and others. Letting go allows you to experience what is possible to receive instead of focusing on what you are not getting. In business, it means understanding that, although someone may not see the same opportunity in business you do, they may be able to refer you to someone they know who can. It means being spontaneous in the moment and asking for the referral, being open to receive the good that is there. Letting go means redirecting the energy that used to be consumed by anger, hurt, and resentment to create the positive outcome you desire. It means forgiving in the moment to receive the good of the situation.

Forgiveness does not mean that you become the world's doormat. Especially in business, it is imperative that you determine the boundaries you will not allow anyone to cross. Forgiveness is an internal emotional experience. You choose forgiveness to release the psychological and emotional distance between you and the positive results you desire. You have the right to neutralize situations that could potentially hurt you by continually exercising boundaries that feel right to you, while letting go of the hurt and resentment connected to your past.

Forgiveness allows you to begin new relationships with a clean slate. Forgiveness allows you to attract positive, productive people to your business and to your life that you can connect and collaborate with. Forgiveness allows you to change the pathway of the neurons in your brain and to create a new biological magnetism to attract people of like mind.

Yes, forgiveness is an internal process that allows you to let go and receive the results you desire and deserve.

Notes

_____

_____

_____

_____

_____

_____

_____

_____

_____

_____

_____

_____

_____

_____

_____

_____

_____

_____

_____

_____

_____

Notes

_____

_____

_____

_____

_____

_____

_____

_____

_____

_____

_____

_____

_____

_____

_____

_____

_____

_____

_____

_____

_____

8

THE POWER OF CREATIVITY

In addition to your uniqueness, your creativity is one of the most valuable attributes you bring to the marketplace as an entrepreneur. Creativity is the ability to create an idea, product, service, or strategy rather than imitate one which already exists. Your creative ability is very powerful because it enables you to invent a new reality from your vision in your imagination. You become the creator of your enterprise and the designer of your life, bringing your unique ideas to fruition through the results you create.

We Are All Creative

Each and every one of us has creativity within us. Each of us drew pictures, painted masterpieces, built fortresses, created imaginary friends, or expressed the vividness of our imagination in some way as a child. We played house, played telephone, sang songs and told stories, played with dolls or action figures, and engaged in many other activities that expressed our fantasies and internal visions. As children, we were free in our expression of the visions in our minds until we learned that they were not appreciated, valued, or approved of by someone else as we grew up. If our dreams or imaginations were stifled by someone whose approval we sought, we learned very quickly to keep our ideas to ourselves, and soon we lost touch with much of our creativity.

Being creative means having the courage to believe in your insights, to intuitively transition to the next step, and to take risks, even if you are not confident of the outcome. As an entrepreneur, it is important that you learn to use your creativity to reinvent yourself and your enterprise when an idea or strategy does not yield the anticipated result. As you begin to apply your ideas in practical ways to produce results, you will find that it is often necessary to reinvent the way the idea is applied to yield the result you desire. This means existing in a constant state of creative transformation. I am not suggesting that you will be recreating yourself entirely every moment of every day, but you must have enough vision and flexibility to trust your intuitive impulses when an inspiration flashes into your mind. This means being free to follow a whim when that tiny voice inside you beckons you to change your strategy midstream and go against the status quo. When you honor your personal impulse and follow it where it leads, letting go of the need for external validation or approval, creativity is born.

Reconnecting to Your Creativity

Creativity is not only for those we consider geniuses to experience. As a human being, you too have creative ability within you. We are all born creative; we just forget how to connect to the inspiration within us. We get conditioned to exist in the frantic hustle and bustle of survival in a world where our senses are constantly bombarded with input almost every moment of every day. Reconnecting with your creative self will require you to reconnect with the peace within you, to stay centered and to observe and listen to yourself. Creativity requires a quieting of your busy mind in order to silence the input of the world around you. This allows you to reconnect with the world within you, which is where your creativity lies.

Reconnecting with your creativity, uniqueness and brilliance is also going to require that you release your impulse to judge your ideas as soon as they come to mind. The average person has heard the word "no" from their parents approximately 144,000 times by the time they turn eighteen. No wonder it becomes automatic to think "that would never work" when struck by a new idea or inspiration.

It is only in the absence of judgment that an idea or creative impulse can ever flourish and grow to fulfill its complete potential.

Your ideas and impulses are what you get paid for in free enterprise. You will unequivocally achieve more results being outrageous than you ever will by following the herd, doing what is perceived as acceptable by society. It is the few who dare to break free from the confines of the rules of society who gain the fame and fortune that so many of us seek to achieve. Outrageousness does not necessarily mean being outlandish. Being outrageous can be as simple as choosing a paint color for a room in your house that no one else in your family would ever dare to use. It may mean becoming athletic when you were told your entire life that you had no athletic ability. Being outrageous means giving yourself permission to break free of the confines that have been keeping you average. Once again, it means having the courage to be different than you have been conditioned to be. It means diving into the pool of inspiration rather than testing the temperature of the water with your big toe to determine if it is going to be comfortable to slip in.

Reconnecting to your creativity can be accomplished in just a few minutes a day. Create five to fifteen minutes where you can be quiet and relax into silence. If you find yourself becoming distracted by thoughts of all that is left unfinished or must still be accomplished, relax and observe your thoughts. Learn to say, "That is interesting, but now is the time for peace in my mind." Release your internal critic and censor and simply observe and experience the thoughts and ideas that manifest. It is often the ideas that seem silly at first which provide the greatest insight and wisdom.

Focus on what inspires you during this time. Consider the books or magazines you read, the people you desire to converse with, the projects you seek to begin in your leisure time, the places you would like to travel to, your dreams, your aspirations, and your desires. Select a vehicle for recording your creative images, thoughts, ideas, and emotions. This could be writing, painting, drawing, or singing. Honor all of your thoughts and ideas. This trust in your creative process will connect you with your creative voice.

It is this voice that can connect you with the brilliant ideas within you that can change your life.

Be Part of a Mastermind Team

It is also important as you develop your creativity that you connect with other individuals on the same path as you in your journey. These are like-minded individuals you can mastermind with to enhance the value of your ideas or creations. A Mastermind Team is a group of such individuals who share ideas and support each other through the entrepreneurial process. These are people you can brainstorm with; people who do not require you have a complete action plan in place when you share you idea in order to understand its brilliance.

My husband, Jeff, is an integral person on my Mastermind Team. I can share the spark of an idea with him, and he can instantly envision all of the great results that can be created with that one idea. In turn, he can share a moment of brilliance with me as well, and then we collaborate to bring our mutual visions to reality. This unconditional support of each other allows us to not only be connected to our creativity much more of the time, but has also created a nonjudgmental forum for each of us to share our ideas with each other.

The Four Phases of Creativity

A Mastermind Team can provide you with the support you deserve to have the courage to capitalize on your brilliance. It also acts as a validation that you are not in fact crazy and that realizing your dreams is not only possible, but definite. There are four phases to capitalizing on creativity: *possible, probable, likely* and *definite*.

If you're like most people, you usually begin in the *possible* phase when you first recognize a creative or brilliant idea within you. There is a possibility that the idea could work, but you have no idea how yet. The *probable* phase of creativity occurs when you begin to create a system or method to manifest your idea. It is the foundation to realizing your dream or vision. As the practical application of your idea takes shape, you transition into the *likely* phase of creativity. This means you have put this idea into some form of application and begun to experience some tangible evidence that yes, this can work! The final phase of creativity is *definite*. Here you operate from the perspective of "I will not be denied." You decide you are willing to sort through the masses of society to find the classes of people who see the same vision as you, and finally connect with the few who are ready to embark on your journey with you. This is when if 200 publishers tell you your book will not sell, you decide to self-publish. This is when you go into fifth gear or entrepreneurial overdrive to create an opportunity rather than waiting for it.

As you connect with your creativity, be aware of who you are sharing your ideas with. Are the people on your Mastermind Team prosperous or struggling? Are they achieving the results in life that you seek to achieve? Are they big dreamers? Are they tenacious in the pursuit of their dreams? I see so many people who share their ideas with people who are not in a position to see the same vision and then become discouraged as a result. Sometimes you might outgrow your original Mastermind Team if you are growing and developing faster than they are. You always want to be in a position where you are sharing your ideas with people who have bigger goals than you do. Not only will they provide the most support for you on your journey, they will also have ideas of their own that you might capitalize on. Together, you begin creating a mutual passion for manifesting your dreams and capitalizing on the brilliance within you.

The Courage to Be Creative

When your passion for your ideas outweighs your anxiety that they may not pan out, you will begin to take calculated risks for reward. There is no reward without the investment of some risk, whether the risk is financial or emotional. Think of a time when you wanted something so much that you were willing to do anything to get it. You decided you would not be denied. What was the outcome of this experience? Do you feel this same passion for your entrepreneurial endeavor? What are you willing to endure to promote and experience your passion? What is your greatest anxiety about what could happen? Is this anxiety based on real life experience and proof, or are you being distracted by the "what ifs" of your internal critic? Are you willing to accept this limiting belief and deny your passion?

Anxiety is normal, especially in the face of that which is not familiar. Take a moment to visualize yourself on a seesaw. See your enterprise as the fulcrum, with your passion on one end and your anxiety on the other. Take note of how balanced or imbalanced the seesaw is. Now, place yourself on the anxiety side of the seesaw and imagine yourself being outweighed by the passion on the other end of the board, sending you up high. Imagine all of your anxiety sliding down the board, being released and neutralized, allowing your passion to rise and join you in your exhilaration at the top of the board. Spend a few moments in this space and imagine how it would feel to live in this experience of creativity and potency. This seesaw image can assist you to stay connected with your creativity and purpose, as well as assist you when you are faced with choices that might impact the manifestation of your dreams.

Simply engaging in this visual exercise requires creativity! If you have doubted your creative ability, let this be an anchor and a foundation for the rest of your creative journey. Capitalizing on your ideas as an entrepreneur requires that you first create the space and permission to acknowledge your ideas as valid, even if some seem outrageous at first. After all, it is the desire to design an exceptional life rather than settle for an average living that led you to free enterprise in the first place.

Notes

_____

_____

_____

_____

_____

_____

_____

_____

_____

_____

_____

_____

_____

_____

_____

_____

_____

_____

_____

_____

Notes

_____

_____

_____

_____

_____

_____

_____

_____

_____

_____

_____

_____

_____

_____

_____

_____

_____

_____

_____

_____

_____

_____

_____

_____

9

THE POWER OF INTUITION

What is intuition? It is an inner knowing, an innate sense of certainty, a hunch, a premonition, a gut feeling, and most importantly, a very important contributor to the way decisions are created. Have you ever just *known* something without being able to explain how you arrived at your conclusion? Have you ever just *felt* you knew the outcome of an event or situation without being able to explain why? Have you ever finished someone's sentence for them or just felt you knew what they were about to say next, and then they said those exact words a few seconds later? Intuition can be defined as an inner sense of truth and is closely connected to our creativity. Successful people are often very intuitive and follow their gut feelings. This internal communication creates a sense of flow, and contributes to a very alive, productive, and desirable state of consciousness.

Your intuition is your inner sense that tells you what feels right and what is true for you in any given moment. It is a source of knowledge and deep wisdom that resides in each and every one of us. When accessed, your intuition allows you to tap into your inner knowing and acknowledge the legitimacy of your feelings as well as your rational thoughts. We live in a society that places a tremendous amount of importance on logical and rational thought and problem solving. We focus almost exclusively on developing our left-brain, rational abilities and pay very little attention to our right-brain, intuitive, emotional, and creative capacity.

Balancing Both Sides of Your Brain

Your left brain, or rational mind, is very much like a computer. It processes the input it receives and calculates logical conclusions based on this information. Your rational mind can only process the data it receives from the external world, operating on the direct experience you have had in your lifetime and the knowledge you have gained through your five senses. Your right brain, or intuitive mind, seems to have an inexhaustible supply of information, including information you have not gathered through your own personal experience. It has the ability to sort through all of this data and supply you with the exact information you require in the exact moment you require it. This is when you make a decision simply because "it feels right" even if it does not make perfect logical sense.

It is important that you begin to create a balance between your rational mind and your intuitive mind. Most people have trained themselves to discount their intuition, but it is your intuition that will lead you to new opportunities or allow you to create new situations in your enterprise. Intuitive decisions often appear as gentle nudges, urging you in the direction you should follow. Haven't you ever heard someone say, "If only I had followed my gut and purchased that stock before it split!" or "I knew I should not have bet on that team!" These are prime examples of discounted intuition. By balancing the attention you place on both your rational and intuitive minds, you will begin to create a foundation of experience to improve your intuitive skills.

The Importance of Intuitive Skills

Why is developing your intuition so important? Intuitive skills will assist you to:

- Size up situations more quickly and with more ease
- Feel confident that the first solution you create is a good one
- Develop a good sense of what will happen next
- Avoid analysis paralysis (being consumed by overwhelming data)
- Remain calm in the face of pressure and uncertainty

- Create alternative solutions when a plan runs into unforeseen challenges
- Create decisions in the moment to move on to more productive situations

Intuitive Decision-Making

As an entrepreneur, you will be faced with multiple situations each and every day which require quick decisions to capitalize on the moment. Jeff and I own four businesses, and if we stopped all momentum to rationally analyze each and every situation that occurs on a daily basis in each company we would never have any time or energy left to produce! Intuitive decision-making requires you to act upon a reflex. It means that you experience internal emotional feedback in response to a situation or challenge and then create a solution or decision reflexively. This requires becoming much more in tune with how you feel and less connected to what you think.

In free enterprise, thinking is overrated. It is much more important that, when presented with an opportunity, you are connected with the instant emotional response of "Wow, I'd love to do this! This really feels right for me!" All too often, we stop to think and analyze, while opportunity continues to move. When we are finally ready to decide, we find that opportunity has passed us by. Have you ever heard the adage "Dogs only bark at moving cars?" As a business owner, this means opportunity is only created by a business in motion. How would relying on your intuition assist you to pick up the pace of your enterprise to create more momentum around you?

Developing Your Intuitive Ability

Developing your intuitive ability begins with increasing your awareness of what is happening emotionally inside of you so that you can capture these inner dialogues when they are happening or shortly thereafter. Becoming more aware of your internal processes will allow you to acknowledge intuitive feelings as they pop up so you can access them consciously as well as subconsciously. Intuition is a natural process, one that we are all born with, and it is predominant in children. As we experience life, we are usually conditioned to turn these feelings off or discount them in the face of logical thinking or rational explanations. Reconnecting to and trusting your intuitive abilities requires repetition and experience but is actually easier than you may perceive.

Many athletes tune into their intuition while competing in their sport, just as many speakers, authors, and performers tune into their intuition in their most brilliant or creative moments. If you stop to consider your experiences, I'm sure you can also recognize moments of intuition you have had but perhaps discounted or ignored. For instance, in school, did you ever feel that the teacher was going to call on you and then she did? Have you ever worried that a potential business partner would ask you how long you have been involved in your particular industry only to receive the exact question you dreaded answering? Have you ever just felt that you were about to have a phenomenal day and then be surprised by a huge windfall you were not expecting?

Most successful people follow their gut feelings when making business and investment decisions. Thomas Edison is a great example of following intuition as he first dreamed of the light bulb, and then proceeded to invent one. Mark Victor Hansen is another great example of the importance of following your intuition. Mark is the cocreator of the *Chicken Soup for the Soul* series, a book he originally self-published because the publishing houses he approached with his idea told him it would never sell in a bookstore. It's a good thing he trusted his gut instead of the critical evidence he was receiving about the validity of his idea, because that one idea has gone on to produce more than one billion dollars of intellectual property.

Often our intuitional feelings are so ordinary and mundane that we don't pay any attention to them or do not consider them intuition. For instance, you may be in the middle of a meeting or social event and suddenly feel the urge to leave and hurry home or leave the room to check your cell phone. Immediately, another voice is triggered inside your head that says, "Don't be ridiculous! You can't leave now! Everyone will be staring at you!" So instead of following your gut feeling, you stay in a situation you don't really want to be in, and find out later that you missed a crucial phone call, or that had you left a few moments earlier your path would have crossed that of someone of influence and affluence you had been looking forward to meeting. When we follow our intuition, we often do not know exactly what we are doing or why, but there are often some surprising and interesting results we receive to validate our behavior.

In general, when we follow our true intuitive feelings, situations seem to resolve themselves, although it is often not in the way we planned or expected. These resolutions allow us to feel energized and alive in the moment, creating a sense of being in the flow of life. When we do not follow our intuition, we can often feel depressed, repressed, blocked, and out of flow, as if life is a force acting against us instead of us experiencing life.

The key here is to learn to follow your intuition, even if it does not accommodate the people around you. In our society, it is so common to be conditioned from an early age to take into consideration the requirements of those around us and to follow certain rules of behavior, suppressing our spontaneous impulses, to ensure everyone else is fulfilled before we seek our own fulfillment. We learn to look to outside authorities for permission, answers, and direction, rather that looking inward for the answers. This is exactly why I teach that success in free enterprise requires a different level of permission than we are taught by society. The only permission you require is your own, and as long as you look to others for your answers, you will limit your results. Until you learn to trust yourself and your own inner authority, you will be limited in the results you create and the life you experience.

Stop Giving Away Your Power

It is time to drop the drama of giving your power away to outside authorities in exchange for their approval if you want to live your dreams. The only permission you require to succeed is your own, so at what point will you give yourself that permission? This is tapping into your inner knowing about where you are headed and why. This is where you begin to identify and live your purpose. This is where you are in your enterprise and your enterprise is in you. How can you be in alignment with what you seek if your actions are dependent on the permission of anyone other than yourself?

Letting go of the information from people around you requires that you allow your body and mind to relax enough so that you allow your attention to move out of your head and down into the core of your body. Your power lies between your belly button and your groin—the same place your gut feelings reside.

In this modern world, we become so accustomed to operating under stress that we forget how to relax. We are constantly so bombarded by noise, information, emotions, commercials, chemicals, and other external stimuli that we do not realize the state of stress our bodies and minds are in the majority of the time. This is why most people toss and turn while they sleep—they have not learned how to relax and release the stresses of the day that has passed. This is also why many people simply fall asleep when they first experiment with meditation. Connecting with your intuition requires you to relax physically, mentally, and emotionally, even if only for a moment at first. This is where you will find your peace. Your peace lies in the moments when the information and demands of the world around you cease to harbor any of your attention. Your intuition will speak the most clearly and definitely in these moments. The more you create these moments for yourself, the more time you will be able to spend in this state. It is an emotional and physical state where you are able to respond to life in the moment rather than react based on all of your past experiences. This is where your intuitive guidance is leading you consistently toward the resolutions you seek rather than the confrontations you would prefer to avoid.

When you become more comfortable with your internal dialogue, you will begin to allow yourself to say what you feel rather than what you perceive the perfect response to be. When you are able to operate from this perspective, life becomes much easier because you are once again in the flow rather than resisting the current. Being in the flow of life is much more about being in tune with your emotional reality than it is flowing with what is happening around you. If your circumstances do not harmonize with your emotions, then you probably discounted an intuitional premise that has already occurred.

The Role of Intuition in Free Enterprise

Intuition is not an exact science. It is a sense and a skill which will be different for each of us. It is also a key to capitalizing on opportunity as an entrepreneur. The word *entrepreneur* literally means "first in." If you are the first in with no factual proof to legitimize the experience, then how can you rationally expect to receive a result? The answer is you can't. When you are leading the pack, you learn to go with your gut and address life as you experience it. If you are not leading the pack, then you are only traveling as fast as the lead horse, and while your experience may be positive and the results fruitful, there is never any great reward without an element of risk. This is where your intuition plays a key role in whether you go for the unknown or stay where the business is safe. The choice will always be up to you.

Notes

Notes

_____

_____

_____

_____

_____

_____

_____

_____

_____

_____

_____

_____

_____

_____

_____

_____

_____

_____

_____

_____

_____

10

THE POWER OF INTEGRITY

Integrity is a character trait that will greatly enhance your odds for long-term success in free enterprise. Integrity means being able to walk your talk. I am sure you have heard the saying "It does not matter if you can talk the talk, what matters is if you can walk the walk." Taking this adage one step further, I believe that it is important to keep our business transactions in alignment with our personal morals and ethical codes, as well as to create an awareness of what is actually happening in reality as opposed to our intentions. Walking your talk means that your actions in business align with your moral principles and that you scrutinize yourself and your business practices as scrupulously as you do the companies you do business with. It is very easy to criticize another business' policies and procedures, especially when they do not create the results you desire as a customer. As a business owner, it is now your responsibility to look objectively in your mirror to ensure that you are aware of how your enterprise is actually operating.

When you own your own enterprise, your personal integrity as well as the integrity of your business will greatly enhance your odds of being successful. One of the benefits of starting your own business is that you have the opportunity to create a company that operates by the principles you believe in. Your business can operate as efficiently and as ethically as you desire. You have the opportunity to create an enterprise that actually delivers the results you have been seeking as a customer from other businesses. Have you ever purchased a product from a company whose customer service was less than satisfactory? In the era of phone trees and automated systems, you have the opportunity to recreate the human experience within your business. Once you have set the ethical structure of your organization, its effectiveness, which applies to all human realms, can be learned. This comes from being conscious of how you use your time, leveraging your natural strengths, prioritizing, and learning to make better decisions.

Operating within your integrity is important because it requires far too much energy to maintain the façade that is created to legitimize your enterprise to the world when you are not in your integrity. I assist entrepreneurs every day who expect their collaborators to take action that they are not willing to take and then wonder why no one is producing. I also assist entrepreneurs who have found a way to dodge the system to create results. They end up making shaky and shady business decisions because they buy into the opportunity to receive short-term results without first considering the possible long-term ramifications. Then they spend enormous amounts of time creating the illusion of legitimacy and end up exhausted. The simplest way to succeed is to operate within your integrity. You may not always create the fastest results, but I guarantee the results you achieve will create a strong foundation to support your enterprise when it flourishes.

Use Integrity to Create Your Niche

The number one reason businesses lose clients is the inability to follow through and deliver what they promise. One of the easiest ways to create a niche for yourself in free enterprise is simply saying what you will do and doing what you say. You want to create a niche you can produce and flourish in because this is what will separate you from your competition. Reliability is a very good niche to establish and maintain. It will also create a unique value for your enterprise because doing what you say is the epitome of great customer service. When you become known for outstanding customer service and absolute reliability, clients, revenue, and opportunity will flow to you abundantly and effortlessly. You will receive great referrals and get exposure to large networks of people because your commodity is so rare. Suddenly, the price of your product or service becomes irrelevant, because the value you are providing through your service is unequalled in your market.

The Art of Under-Promising and Over-Delivering

You want to learn the art of under-promising and over-delivering. It is a very human quality to desire to "wow" your consumers and to promise them the moon and the stars to do so. The challenge with this impulse is that you put yourself in a position where it becomes impossible to deliver what you promised. Your clients will be more impressed when you exceed their expectations than they ever will be when you just meet them. It is time to become more practical in your desire to please your buyers or collaborators. You want to make sure that the promises you make to your buyers can be reasonably fulfilled, creating room to succeed and be the hero instead of promising results you cannot reasonably fulfill, letting your customer down and leaving you feeling like a zero.

Remember, what is pleasurable is what we do! Begin structuring your enterprise in ways that allow you to enjoy the entrepreneurial process. Create expectations for your collaborators and clients that are easily met so that when you go the extra mile it is easy for them to recognize that you have so they can express their appreciation. Here is a very simple example of what I mean: Jeff and I take great pride in providing exceptional customer service to our clients. One way we do this is by responding to all of our phone calls and emails, as well as shipping all orders, within twenty-four hours. I will often respond to an email within minutes of receiving it, and will often simply call the client if my response would be expressed better verbally than in a written reply. Not a day goes by where I do not hear someone say, "I can't believe you actually called me back!" My answer is always the same, "Why? Don't you feel you deserve a response?"

One-on-one personal attention and customer service is practically unheard of in today's business world, especially from the president or vice-president of a corporation. And yet, without our clients there would be no corporation. When you apply the Golden Rule to your enterprise, treating others as you wish to be treated, you create an entirely different experience for yourself and your consumers and collaborators.

Seven Characteristics of Integrity

Here are seven simple characteristics of integrity to consider when evaluating yourself and your enterprise:

Release the Urge to Imitate

It can be very appealing to copy or imitate what you perceive to be a flourishing enterprise in your industry, just as often it is enticing to imitate the style, haircut, or image of someone you admire. I call this "the grass is always greener" mentality, meaning "If only I were more _____, then _____ would be less effort." Let me be the first to tell you that when you judge a book by its cover you miss a lot of the internal content. An image is exactly that —a premeditated display of what someone or another company wants you to see—their glorious façade. There is nothing wrong with this either; it is also known as putting your best foot forward. We all do this and since we never get a second chance to make a first impression, we will continue this practice.

Resist the temptation to criticize and judge yourself or your enterprise based on your perception of another person or another enterprise. Success is not a competitive race, with one winner and many losers. Success is a process, and as an entrepreneur you have the opportunity to finally receive the recognition for your brilliance you have always sought, provided you remain genuine as you go through the process. Your uniqueness is the intrinsic spiritual value you bring to life, and this is what can allow your enterprise to produce massive results.

Celebrating your uniqueness allows you to be genuine in your collaborations and allows you to attract clients who recognize and value you for who you are. It is so much easier to relax and produce from your genuineness than it ever is to maintain a veneer disguising the real you. The same goes for your enterprise. You may not always top the charts in expansion, growth, or revenue, but your enterprise can always operate within your integrity so that you can feel good about the results you do achieve.

Set the Standard Instead of Rising to Meet It

Every industry has a standard of quality that is deemed acceptable in the marketplace. Take pride in your enterprise, your product, and your service. Create a conscious choice to become a leader in your industry by setting the standard of excellence, rather than settling for consumer acceptance. This will require vision, creativity, and the belief that you are able to create in reality what you see in your vision, even though it has never been done before, period, or it hasn't been done in the way you are envisioning. Stimulating your creativity and vision requires you to disconnect from the noise of day-to-day living. This will require time away from your television, radio, and even time away from family and friends if their vision is not as encompassing as yours. Create an arena where you can excel in your industry, even if only in one aspect. If you are willing to provide yourself with this space and permission to flourish, your rewards will greatly outweigh your sacrifices.

Thomas Edison attempted more than 10,000 different applications of his vision before his creativity "tuned in" on the right combination to perfect the incandescent light. He experienced a similar experience when he created the phonograph.

On your journey, you will attract both supporters and naysayers. It is your choice whose input you resonate with. Setting the standard requires your courage to cling to the top of the ladder, which is never crowded, and then to deliver the message of what you see to those clinging to the rungs below you. Be prepared for some fall out and attrition. This is the part of the process of capitalizing on your brilliance. Be willing to let the opinions of others go so you can pursue your dreams. I guarantee that when you release your emotional connection to the masses, you will begin to attract the classes, and it is through the classes that you can set a new standard of excellence.

Truth – Why We Perceive It Hurts

Who created the idea of "brutal honesty"? Why do we as a society resist the idea of candidness and sincerity when we conversely complain of living in a world of corruption and deception? Why do we resist taking an objective look into our emotional mirrors when we already know what our reflections will reveal?

One of the greatest fallacies we create as humans is the idea that we have perfected any one aspect of our existence. I have learned in my own growth and development that is just when I am feeling smug and satisfied with my knowledge or insight about a certain situation that I receive an encounter or situation to completely negate my position and am very effectively removed from my soapbox. The book you are reading is a great example of this very situation. In 2005, I noticed that there were very few books written for women about entrepreneurial success. I decided to create a book to change this situation based on my own growth and entrepreneurial experience. About halfway through my writing process, I paralyzed my creative flow with the worry that I might lose my identity if my book were the success Jeff and I perceived it could be. I began to doubt my ability, my information, and most of all, my desire to produce a book to empower women. I wanted to inspire women to create changes, but felt more comfortable doing so if I could inspire them from stage left, well out of the way of the spotlight.

The truth was that I was already anticipating a tremendous amount of pressure from the success of my book before it was even written. There is no guarantee that this book will become a national best seller, and if it does, I reserve the right to create decisions that serve me, regardless of the pressure to perform. After six weeks of procrastination and denial, I allowed myself to be honest and to recognize what was staunching my creative flow. The moment I acknowledged the truth behind my "writer's block," I ceased to have writer's block. Was this brutal? Of course not! This was one of the most liberating epiphanies of my development! I realized that no matter what the pressure or demand created by my book's success, or no matter what the ramifications of my book's mediocrity, because I am creating my experience I reserve the right to make the choices that serve me, even if this means saying "no."

The truth can absolutely set you free emotionally, and it is your emotions that act as your cause, driving the effect of either your action or inaction. It is time for you to be honest with yourself abut why you seek entrepreneurial success and what you will do if your dreams manifest, as well as what you will do if they do not. Regardless of our brilliance, there are no guarantees in this world. The only situations we can rely on are those we create through our emotional dialogue with ourselves, and the emotional expectations we create and expect to experience in return. Understanding your motivations and perceived pressures can also allow you to stop taking yourself so seriously. One of the most liberating experiences I have created is to laugh at myself when my emotional expectations are overwhelming my current experiences. This requires the courage to be honest with myself, not only recognizing my feelings, but also determining if they are in alignment with what is really happening around me. This is the truth of experience; when you can look at life from this perspective with a level of objectivity, your pressure to perform perfectly can be released and your permission to be yourself and to consciously create your experiences can be revealed.

Learning for Life

Have you ever noticed that just when you feel you have a particular situation all figured out, life throws you a curve ball as if to prove to you how little you actually understand? Regardless of your entrepreneurial experiences, sales skills or ability to communicate with people, you will find that free enterprise is a process of continuing education.

Life is in a constant state of transition and it is only your perception that makes you believe that a situation is static. The more you continue to grow and develop, the easier it typically is to stay in the flow of life's transitions. It is your willingness to receive the information from each experience and incorporate this information into your awareness that allows you to stay in the flow of your own evolution.

Your willingness to learn, grow, and change will enhance your experience, not only as an entrepreneur, but also as a human being. There will always be someone who has had more experience or created more results in your entrepreneurial arena. This is the exact person whose collaboration or mentorship would allow you to progress toward your goals more effortlessly. It is natural to resist learning from someone we perceive as competition, but when you allow yourself to stop comparing yourself and your results to others, you will find that there is never any competition in collaboration. Your willingness to learn from someone else also opens the door for them to receive valuable information from you in return. Success is a collaborative process; you require the support, knowledge, and skills of other people to create a flourishing enterprise.

The moment you feel resistance to connecting with someone you can learn from, you want to check in with yourself and ask, "Is this resistance in alignment with my integrity?" Stop for a moment to consider if this person in your present reality reminds you of someone from your past, both physically and emotionally. When you have made this connection, forgive your past experience that would sabotage your present opportunity, and let it go. Consciously connect with the person or information you can receive to continue your entrepreneurial education. The game of free enterprise offers no finish line, and the school of knowledge offers no diploma or graduation date. In this game you are offered the opportunity for success through your experiences in the process and the insights you gain there. The more you are willing to learn, grow, and change, the easier it will be to travel this journey and to stay in your integrity.

Knowing When Not to Compromise

In a compromise, both parties mutually concede to create a resolution satisfactory to both. In a true compromise, each party concedes something the other side finds acceptable. A compromise does not always create a win-win situation, but it does create space to move forward. Business requires compromise; the ability to negotiate a "yes" is a valuable skill to develop.

It is also important that you understand where your boundaries lie in business. You will learn this through repetition and experience as you develop your enterprise, but it is also necessary to determine where your lines are drawn in accordance to your ethics. These are the lines that, regardless of the situation, you will not cross; you will not compromise your moral and ethical code.

Developing this code in your enterprise will assist you to stay in your integrity as an entrepreneur just as it does in your personal life. When you are conscious of these boundaries, you will learn to gracefully withdraw from potentially controversial situations. The more controversy you are able to neutralize or avoid, the less you will attract drama and chaos to your business.

Defining Your Values

Defining your values is one of the key components to integrity. Values develop out of our emotional connection to our experiences with people who are important to us, particularly our parents. Understanding your values and how you created them is imperative as an entrepreneur, because your values are what allow you to create sound, consistent decisions. Your decisions will either create progression, regression, or stagnation in your enterprise. You may find that the values established in your childhood require examination and restructuring to serve you now in free enterprise.

Being aware of your values creates clarity for you to connect with other people who have the same values you do. When your intrinsic values are in alignment with the people you do business with, creating results you feel good about is effortless.

Responsibility

Responsibility generally gets a bad rap in our society because it is typically viewed as an obligation, a charge, a burden, and a duty. Most of us have been accused of irresponsibility at one point in time, and received some form of repercussion as a result.

Responsibility is defined as "the ability to respond." In any given situation you have options to choose from to determine your response. Your response creates an outcome—another situation to respond to. Free enterprise will require you to acknowledge how your response contributes to the outcome of the situations you encounter. When you can objectively hold yourself accountable for your role in any given situation, you will find you are able to respond with very little effort.

Business requires quick decisions, and most people will hesitate before deciding because they are anxious about the result of their decisions. Have faith that you are capable of responding to any situation you create, whether you receive the results you intended or not. Now that you are all grown up, you are fully capable and qualified to respond to life!

I have created a list of questions to consider as you examine your integrity. Self-analysis is essential to your entrepreneurial progress because it shows you where you are progressing and where your development requires some additional attention. Your effectiveness in the marketplace will increase through progress, even if your progress is slow in the beginning. Each aspect of your personal development will progress at a different rate. It is the small, consistent actions repeated over time that lead to quantum leap results!

Questions for Self-Analysis:

Are my goals and objectives for this week/month/quarter/year realistically attainable based on my skills and experience?

Am I delivering service to the best quality I am capable, or can I improve any part of my service?

Am I delivering the quantity of service I am capable of?

Does my business attitude portray gratitude for my entrepreneurial experience?

Does procrastination inhibit my efficiency? If so, to what extent?

Do I complete what I begin?

Are my decisions created in the moment with confidence?

Is my guilt from my past or my anxiety about the future affecting my results?

Is my energy focused on revenue-producing activity?

Am I open to receiving feedback to assist my development?

How have I improved my ability to create service and value?

How can I change the way I use my time to become more effective?

Does my conduct toward my associates and clients induce the respect I seek?

Are my business decisions in alignment with my conscience?

If I were to collaborate with or purchase from me, would I find the experience satisfying?

Am I in the right vocation? If not, why? What would I rather pursue?

What have you learned through this analysis? The purpose of this exercise is to create a very clear picture of where you have progressed and where you require development. With this clarity you can determine if your perception of your personal development and entrepreneurial effectiveness aligns with your results. You may find that your results exceed your perception or perhaps you have perceived a higher level of effectiveness than your results indicate. Perhaps your self-analysis has returned exactly the information you expected to receive. Regardless of your discovery, this exercise is a very effective method of checking in with your integrity periodically as you continue your journey in free enterprise.

Notes

_____

_____

_____

_____

_____

_____

_____

_____

_____

_____

_____

_____

_____

_____

_____

_____

_____

_____

_____

Notes

11

THE POWER OF PRODUCTION

As you have experienced, or have begun to realize, entrepreneurs get paid for results, not time. This is one of the most valuable situations you can come to terms with, and it is also one of the major keys to entrepreneurship that keeps most people stuck in their businesses. As employees, we are quickly conditioned to trade our time for dollars, settling for a wage that is based on what our employer has decided the task we perform on a daily basis is worth. As entrepreneurs, we have the opportunity to receive as much as the free market will bear in return for our energy, but our energy must be transmuted into a tangible product or service that creates enough perceived value that other people will buy it.

A Simple Recipe for Entrepreneurial Success

The simple entrepreneurial equation is: $D + A - (EE) = R$

Decision + Action − (Emotional Expectation) = Results

In this equation, Decision is your reason for bringing you proposed product to the marketplace, otherwise known as your "Why." Action is what you are required to do in order to receive a return on your idea (i.e., how you will market your product). Emotional Expectation is the time frame you create for the results you expect based on your entrepreneurial experience. Results are created when the components on the left side of the equation fall into alignment. Results can also be called Production.

This is a very simple recipe for entrepreneurial success, yet most entrepreneurs are challenged when it comes to taking action to produce results. In my opinion, one of the reasons struggle is so predominant in the entrepreneurial arena is because we enter this game as adults, bringing with us a lifetime of previous experiences, most of which will not serve us when it comes to creating results in our own enterprises. Unless you had the benefit of growing up in an entrepreneurial family, you were not only conditioned to perform for approval, meaning a grade (in school), but you also watched your parents operate within their jobs, and all of this combined experience will not assist you to succeed in your own enterprise.

I have seen many successful, brilliant businesspeople fail as entrepreneurs, and conversely I have seen the least likely candidate for entrepreneurial success flourish in the right opportunity. This just goes to show that in a free marketplace the only rules that apply are those you create for yourself. It is very simple to see that without production, results, meaning revenue, can be very elusive, meaning not present. Yet production is the exact situation most people both approach and avoid because of their perceptions of what it means and what it will require to achieve results.

Releasing Emotional Expectations

One of the predominant reasons I see people struggle is that their emotional expectation of the results they expect themselves to produce is much too high. They decide to give free enterprise a shot, give it a try, see what happens, and hope for the best without a realistic expectation of the skills they require to create the results they seek in their enterprises. It makes logical sense that with a great product and sound business plan, an enterprise can be up and profitable in ninety days to six months. This is, of course, provided that every single element of your business and marketing plan operates in reality exactly as it prints on paper. Most people never take into account their entrepreneurial experience or lack thereof, or the human predominance toward procrastination, or the overhead required to continue operation while striving to achieve profit.

Most business plans fail to consider the most important part of the equation when determining a business' success or failure in free enterprise, and that commodity is you!

Imagine how much differently you would have created your original expectations of yourself and your performance when considering the opportunity to create results as an entrepreneur if you had only known then what you know now. The great news is that as president, founder and CEO of your own enterprise, you have the opportunity to hire and fire yourself each and every day. You can choose to release your emotional expectations of yourself and begin to enjoy your entrepreneurial journey.

What commonly happens is that we create unrealistic expectations of the results we will produce in a given time frame. When the results do not manifest as we envision, or the profit does not automatically begin to flow into our enterprises, we become disappointed and discouraged. The definition of the word *discouraged* is "not of courage," and you require courage to stay in the game long enough to produce results. As my husband Jeff says in his book *More Heart Than Talent,* courage is a commodity there is always a market for, and it never goes out of style. Success as an entrepreneur requires that you have the courage to constantly reinvent yourself and to stay in the process of transition. Often, it is not the first marketing strategy or product we create that ultimately leads us to our promised land of financial freedom. Success requires the courage to stay in the process of transformation and development in the face of challenges and perceived setbacks. You will probably experience many of these on your journey, as all successful people do. These are not failures, but rather opportunities to gain the knowledge and experience to produce the results that will allow you to change the quality of your life.

As the owner of your own enterprise, you have the opportunity to design your life. You have the opportunity to choose the experiences you will create while you are living rather than simply settle for the circumstances life hands you. It is important that you realize that we are all in a constant state of transition. Each moment of every experience gives us the opportunity to grow or to stagnate. The apparent stability of your situation or the apparent inability to progress is nothing more than an illusion created by your perception of reality. It is easy to become discouraged when the results you desire to produce do not manifest exactly as you expected, especially since we live in a society conditioned to operate within the confines of a job. The idea of free enterprise and entrepreneurship and the pursuit of living your goals and dreams is outside of most people's comfort zone, and they are usually more willing to validate your failed attempts than they ever are to commend your courage for stepping outside of the box of your job to manifest your desires as your reality. Understand that we live in a world that is conditioned to spend a lot of time worrying about problems, such as the war in the Middle East, escalating gas prices, the homeless population, problems with disease, the instability of the job market, etc. When you turn your focus toward the problems of life, it does not matter if the problems directly influence you or your family, or if the situations can be solved by you; either way, they distract your energy from creating change in your present.

Living in the Solution

Producing results in any enterprise requires you to become solution-oriented. This means spending more time living in the solution rather than focusing on your problems. Doing this requires a different level of objectivity to begin to redefine problems as challenges. There is no right or wrong solution to any challenge you will face as an entrepreneur. You have the ability to create a solution based on your experience this far, and then you have the opportunity to learn from the situation created as a result of your action in the moment. Receiving a bill you do not have the money to pay in the moment the bill arrives on your doorstep can be a problem. As a problem, it is easy to perceive yourself as a victim of circumstance, saying to yourself, "How can I pay this? I don't have the money!" Objectively, it is also possible to receive this bill and say to yourself, "I am fortunate as an entrepreneur that I have the opportunity to produce results and attract this money before this bill is due."

The power of production lies in your perception of what you are able to create. It requires a transformation of focus from what you do not currently have to what you have the ability to create. When you can produce results, then struggle—whether financial or emotional—becomes a situation from the past. The ability to produce results also provides the conscious realization that you are in fact capable of flourishing in any given situation. This will require you to take action as if you are already producing the results you seek. A common misconception of our society is that you will not feel successful until you have produced the results that represent success to you. In reality, it is the exact opposite. When you allow yourself to act as if you have already achieved your desired result and feel the fulfillment of success, and when you produce from this emotional perspective, producing results becomes much easier and a whole lot more fun. Once again, when you are able to have fun in your enterprise and in your production it will release your resistance to the actions that create results.

Focus on Revenue-Producing Activities

After all, wouldn't creating more results in your enterprise open a new door to the solutions that would resolve many of your current challenges? Results are what will create the finances to provide you with the leverage to have more options in life; this is why production is so powerful. If you are seeking more results, become more productive with your time. Focus on revenue-producing activity instead of what keeps you busy. There is a time for paperwork, personal development, and research, and that time is after the close of business for the day or early in the morning prior to the beginning of your business day. Shuffling papers, organizing your office, reading books, listening to CDs or tapes, or researching your company, product, or opportunity is not what is going to produce results for you. Connecting with people, marketing yourself, and closing sales are where you should be focusing the majority of your time, especially if you are financially challenged in your enterprise. These are the three main activities that will offer you a return on your energy in a relatively short time frame.

Average entrepreneurs procrastinate and spend a lot of time in nonrevenue-producing activity, while exceptional entrepreneurs jump into the fray and produce. Procrastination is often due to unwarranted perfection, meaning when all your ducks are in a row and your office is totally organized and you have memorized all of the information about your company and product, then you will be ready to produce results. There is validity to all of these situations, but if you allow them to keep you from producing results, you will find that your entrepreneurial progress will feel very slow because it takes you a long time to take action. As an entrepreneur, you receive compensation in direct proportion to your results, not your time. You will not get paid in free enterprise for the time you spend perfecting your expertise and circumstances so that you are in a perfect environment to produce. Most people who get stuck in this cycle of procrastination and unwarranted perfection are so exhausted by the time they are done getting ready to get ready that they have no energy left to produce. As you can see, this is a very self-defeating situation.

As an entrepreneur, you have the opportunity to receive results in return for your energy, provided you invest your energy in revenue-producing activities. This is the return on your investment. The difference between this return on investment and an investment you would make with a financial institution or as a venture capitalist is that now you can directly influence the rate of the return on your energetic investment based on how you spend your time. I guarantee that if you allow yourself to spend more time connecting with people for the next six months, your results will begin to quantify. I see so many people hide in their offices behind their computers and telephones. Yes, we live in a world where communication is greatly enhanced electronically, but the driving commodity in free enterprise is always people: the people you connect with personally and the referrals they bring you. This is about developing a network to enhance your net worth.

Create Great Connections

Creating connections is the name of the game for any business, whether it is brand new or reputable and established. Great people skills will allow you to have an entirely different opportunity to create results than the average person has. People skills are developed through repetition and experience, but most importantly, by learning how to listen. I have found that listening is the key to unlocking the mystery of communicating with other people, because it takes the focus off of you. I have learned to ask more questions during my conversations, and to create situations where I say very little about myself, instead finding out a lot about the person I am talking to. Because we all love to talk about ourselves, the other person leaves feeling like he or she just had a great conversation.

It is very common to feel uncomfortable communicating with someone you do not know because it is natural to worry about how that person will judge or prejudge you. It is also important to realize that your vision of yourself is probably a bit myopic, meaning you have a tendency to see only what you have not done, the success you have not experienced, and the situations you perceive as failures. I guarantee you that no one else would ever pick up on your emotional history if you did not broadcast it during your conversations. Less than twenty percent of how we communicate with each other is expressed through the words we speak. More than eighty percent of our communication is nonverbal, communicated through our tone of voice, body language, and eye contact (or lack thereof).

Last weekend I had the opportunity to observe 600 people at a convention where Jeff spoke. I spent the day at our sales table outside the meeting room, mingling and connecting with the participants who attended this event. It was fascinating to see how receptive people were to conversing with me when I was not behind our sales table. The moment they approached the table, however, almost all of them checked out of the situation. I asked them if they were enjoying the day and they said, "No thanks, I'm just looking," as they looked at the floor, the table, above my head, or at some invisible focal point over my right or left shoulder. I responded, "Since that's not what I asked you, are you receiving value from this event?" They would freeze, make eye contact, and then answer my question. Their first response was a knee-jerk reaction to what they perceived would be a high-pressure sales effort from me. My objective at our sales table is obviously to produce revenue, yet how can this happen if my customers are disconnected from the experience before we have even conversed?

Their initial response was not a rejection of me or a judgment of my ability to communicate. Again, it was a knee-jerk reaction that most people have when approached by a salesperson they perceive is going to attempt to sell them something. Creating results in this situation required that I first be able to see if these customers would allow me to neutralize their preconditioned reactions in order to receive a response to the question I actually asked. Provoking them to stop and listen to the question I actually had asked, rather than allowing them to blow me off based on what they thought they heard me say was a return on my energy; a return on my investment. The revenue was not instantaneous at that point, but I was creating a level of rapport with each person where they knew they could relax and have a conversation with me even if I was behind our table. This experience soon drew others to the table to see what was happening. The energy around our table soon became warmer and more positive, which in turn attracted more people to us to see what was happening. It's a good thing I did not take some of the first reactions I received that day personally. Developing great people skills to produce results requires that you stop creating situations to be personally offended by the reactions of people around you. It requires enough objectivity to understand when someone else's reflexive reaction is not about you, but about them and their emotional history.

The Art of Multitasking

The more you allow yourself to stay focused on production, the faster you will experience the success you seek as an entrepreneur. Often, this will require multitasking in addition to great people skills. It will require you to maximize the action you are capable of taking in a shorter time period. Once again, energy and results are rewarded in this game, not time. I have taught myself how to respond to email and engage in a conversation at the same time. I can listen to a client, respond to the conversation, and type all in the same breath. This has taken over four years of practice to develop this ability. It is invaluable to me, because often a client will request information from me via email and I have the ability to send them the information in the moment and be finished with the situation as we end our dialogue. I do not take notes about what my client wanted, what email address to send the information to, and I do not add the task to my to-do list. Instead, the task at hand is completed in the present moment, allowing me to move on to other revenue-producing activities as soon as we are finished communicating.

This practical application of multitasking skills allows me to create more results in less time. This means more revenue faster.

This should be creating an *aha* moment for you. It is much easier to prosper quickly than slowly. The journey to prosperity demands that you spend a lot of time on the highway of profit before you ever reach your destination. This is one highway with no speed limit and unlimited passing lanes. You can also either drive it or fly it! Are you ready to achieve results in your enterprise? Are you ready to see what the free market will bear in return for your energy? If your answer is yes, then it is time to release your perfection and move into production. It is time to stop buying into your current circumstances and claim your power to create your experience!

Notes

_____

_____

_____

_____

_____

_____

_____

_____

_____

_____

_____

_____

_____

_____

_____

_____

_____

_____

_____

_____

_____

_____

Notes

12

THE POWER OF LEADERSHIP

Go to any bookstore in America, and I guarantee you can find hundreds of books about leadership: its importance, the qualities of a leader, leadership myths, how to become a leader, how to develop leaders, and the list goes on. As president and CEO of your own company, basic leadership skills are required if you seek to develop a team of collaborators who will follow you. Leadership is not an inherited trait, although some people are naturally inclined to lead. It is a developed skill, and for the dedicated few, an art. Leadership ability is not determined by age, race, sex, education, knowledge, financial status, or who you know. Leadership is simply the ability to lead—the ability to influence people to follow you. Success in free enterprise is not just about products, services, and compensation plans; it really comes down to people. Leadership requires heart and compassion as well as purpose, strength, and conviction. What really separates leaders from followers is their awareness and sensitivity to the requirements of other people. And it is this awareness and sensitivity that will influence and inspire people to look to you for direction, guidance, and support.

Leadership is not a position; it is an action. A leader sets the example by choosing a direction, and then stays the course through both challenges and triumphs throughout the journey. Great leaders value their supporters and nurture a positive relationship with them, even when the going gets tough. Your attitude toward the people you lead will inspire their loyalty and earn their respect. Cultivating these relationships is imperative to your success, because without supporters to follow you, your leadership position will only exist in your imagination. People are naturally inclined to follow leaders they perceive are influential; people of influence create change to make a difference because they are different themselves. Successful leadership only occurs when you understand that there is a psychology to it and that the success of your organization happens by design, not by accident.

Connect with Your Vision

Leaders have vision, an inner knowing of where they are headed and what they are creating long before the results have manifested. This vision goes far beyond romancing what is possible or what you hope will happen; this is about trusting yourself and creating a prediction of what is going to happen. Your vision is decision-based, inspiring action to create the momentum required to manifest your desire. All activity results from decisions. Affirmations are important and can definitely enhance your esteem, but without a decision and action, affirmations will not produce results. An affirmation without action is nothing more than a hope that somehow something will change so that tomorrow is different than today. Leaders not only inspire action in others, they take action themselves with the knowledge that deciding to take action is the key to manifesting their dreams.

Take a moment to connect with your vision. This is your purpose, your reason for becoming a great leader. What is the situation you seek to create through your entrepreneurial endeavor? What does it look like? How does it feel? Can you see, smell, and taste your vision? Can you describe it to yourself in crystal clarity? Are you clear about what motivates you to do what you do? If your vision is not clear to you, then it is going to be very challenging to describe it to someone else. The clarity of focus you have when looking at your vision in your imagination is going to have a direct effect on the emotional impact it has on others. The more emotionally connected other people become to your vision, the more motivated they will be to follow you. Your vision does not have to be crystal clear right now in this moment, but begin today to create some clarity in your purpose. It doesn't matter if your vision is small or big, but for others to connect to your dreams of the future, they must be this clear at some point.

While leadership skills require study and development, the principles of leadership are actually quite simple. As a leader, you become a mentor, instilling confidence despite the odds, regardless of circumstances. You encourage your team to take initiative and create solutions proactively, and you teach others to take actions that not only benefit them, but also contribute to your organization as a whole. Your actions set the example you ask your team to follow, never asking anyone to do something you would not be willing to do yourself, thus teaching reality instead of theory.

The Qualities of Great Leaders

Take a moment to consider the qualities you seek in a leader. Several commonly accepted qualities of a leader are ambition, charisma, confidence, initiative, independence, creativity, and a sense of responsibility. As I considered this chapter on leadership, I realized that the topics of the first eleven chapters of this book are all qualities that great leaders possess. These are:

Power

Emotional autonomy—emotional independence—is crucial to success in any endeavor involving other people, especially if you are seeking to lead them. When you are in your power, you will find that you have the ability to influence others to take action; you have the ability to be a strong and inspiring leader. People will begin to gravitate toward you as you resonate with the inner strength and courage they seek to possess.

Belief

Leadership will require you to consider the beliefs and perceptions of those who follow you. Often, their beliefs about you and your effectiveness as a leader will mirror your beliefs about yourself. Your beliefs about yourself, your business, and the marketplace will absolutely impact the results you create. As you become more conscious about your beliefs, you will begin noticing how they shape your reality. Most people go through the mundane activity of life without ever considering that they can change their circumstances. Their beliefs remain subconscious, and they continue to settle for making a living rather than choosing to design a life. Don't underestimate the power of your beliefs. The way you interpret yourself and your world and your expectations of what you will receive as a result of your actions has everything to do with determining your quality of life and your influence as a leader.

Permission

The only permission necessary for you to develop your leadership ability or to succeed in free enterprise is your own. You will learn to celebrate your uniqueness and release your emotional attachment to receiving approval from the people around you. In order to capitalize on your unique self, this requires that you give yourself permission to be different from everyone else. This means you begin living in your authentic self. It means you begin allowing people to experience the person you really are inside instead of playing it safe and hiding behind one of the many masks created by your ego.

Self-Esteem

Self-esteem relates to your feelings about yourself. As you become aware that as a human being you are constantly growing and changing, you'll develop self-acceptance—the ability to approve of yourself as a whole person. As a leader, you will have the opportunity to mentor and assist many members of your team in both of these areas, and it is much easier to do so when you have created a solid foundation in your own internal dialogue. The key to creating self-acceptance is to begin to create realistic expectations about yourself and the world around you. This means creating realistic goals and scenarios which are achievable as you continue the process of growth and development. It means developing new habits of thought and emotion regarding what you experience through repetition and experience now that you are becoming conscious of how your beliefs are created. To accept yourself, you must begin releasing your habits, your patterns of judgment, and your negative self-talk. Realize that this will be a process, not an instantaneous transformation.

Posture

Your posture, your emotional energy, will greatly impact your enterprise and the people and situations you attract. Remember, your emotions dictate your expectations and the Universe rewards you with the experience to edify them. To attract great people to lead, learn to resonate with the message "I am the leader you are looking for." The better you become at understanding the way you resonate and attract, the easier it will be for you to assist your team through this process as well.

Language

Great leaders study language and communication and understand their importance in creating results. Language tells you a lot about the person speaking when you begin to pay attention to the messages behind someone's words. When you begin to hear the emotional meaning behind the words people use, you will begin to communicate on an entirely different level than most people. Your team will begin to notice how you seem to "feel" them and they will be right! Your responses will speak to them emotionally because you will be communicating to their emotional consciousness instead of simply responding to the words they speak. This is where you are able to cut to the chase and get right to the heart of the matter in any conversation without seeming too direct, confrontational, or cold. You also want to develop a language of prosperity and teach this language to your team. Refer back to Chapter Six and create a few Post-It notes you can stick around your home or office to remind you of your new dialogue. This can be a simple one word reminder, such as "Receive!" The more frequently you bring the words you desire to speak to the forefront of your awareness, the easier this transition will be.

Forgiveness

Forgiveness allows you to neutralize the human tendency to redirect the feedback of others as self-criticism. Forgiveness allows you to reclaim your power, whether you are forgiving yourself, another person, or a past experience. As a leader you will be putting yourself in the spotlight of your enterprise. This is a very rewarding place to be, but it also creates a position where you are very susceptible to receiving a lot of feedback. Forgiveness allows you to neutralize your past so that your present business experiences do not trigger overwhelming emotions from your personal experiences. The more objective you can allow yourself to be, the more effective you will be in your business.

Creativity

Creativity is the ability to create an idea, product, service, or strategy rather than imitate one that already exists. Your creative ability is very powerful because it enables you to invent a new reality from your vision using your imagination. You become the creator of your enterprise and the designer of your life, bringing your unique ideas to fruition through the results you create. Being creative means having the courage to believe in your insights, to intuitively transition to the next step, and to take risks, even if you are not confident of the outcome. As an entrepreneur, it is important that you learn to use your creativity to reinvent yourself and your enterprise when an idea or strategy does not yield the anticipated result. This is how you teach your team to step out of the box and away from their comfort zone to take greater risks for greater rewards. When your team sees that you are willing to take a leap of faith and pursue your ideas, they will be inspired to begin pursuing theirs as well.

Intuition

Leaders are often very intuitive and follow their gut feelings. This internal communication creates a sense of flow and contributes to a very alive, productive, and desirable state of consciousness. There are very few organizations more powerful or productive than a team of like-minded individuals collaborating and operating from their intuition. Intuitive leaders have a tendency to attract other intuitive people because they are able to recognize the intuitive ability in others, just as they feel it themselves. When an opportunity to create a decision presents itself, begin asking, "What does my intuition tell me to do?" or "What do I feel the outcome will be?" This is a very simple way to reconnect to your intuition or strengthen your current intuitive abilities.

Integrity

Great leaders will never ask someone else to do anything they are not willing to because this would be out of integrity. When your teammates and clients know that your actions align with your words, they will trust you and your results will compound exponentially through business referrals and repeat buyers. As a leader, be prepared to have your integrity tested from time to time. Remember that actions always speak louder than words and be sure you are responding to challenging situations objectively rather than reacting emotionally. This will require resolve and internal strength, but will also earn the respect and loyalty of your peers.

Production

Leaders are great producers, and they focus on results a great deal of the time. The shortest path from one point to another is always a straight line. Leaders learn to see this path quickly, teach others how to see it, and more importantly, learn how to act upon this path to create more results in less time. As an entrepreneur, you will be compensated for your results, not your time. The more effective you and your organization become as a whole, the more results will flow to all of you. More results means more revenue, more revenue means more options in life, and more options means happier, more productive collaborators.

Evaluate Your Leadership Behavior

Now that you have an in-depth understanding of the key qualities of a leader, ask yourself, "Do I lead in such a way that I would willingly follow myself?" Improving your leadership ability and performance is a result of practical application and actual behavior. Examining a recent leadership experience can assist you to evaluate your leadership skills for that situation. Begin by creating a list of five positive and five negative features of your actual and current leadership behavior.

Positive Leadership Behavior

1.
2.
3.
4.
5.

Negative Leadership Behavior

1.
2.
3.
4.
5.

These ten behaviors are most likely relatively easy to recall if you are examining a current situation. Fewer than ten indicates that you can improve your self-awareness or that you require more leadership experience to evaluate. But if you have fewer than ten features, do not despair! It is still valuable to evaluate your list! Consider your list and remember the reactions and responses of the other people in the situation with you. Creating a similar list of five positive and five negative beliefs or perceptions of your team can assist you in this process. Would their feedback be congruent with your list? If not, why? Where can you increase your awareness of yourself and others to create a more empowering situation for everyone?

The more you are willing to objectively evaluate your leadership abilities and skills, the more quickly you will evolve as an effective leader. A great affirmation I learned from Jeff that has assisted me and will assist you on the road to leadership is, "I am the leader that people are looking for. To my reality I attract quality, like-minded individuals that I can partner with to develop six- and seven-figure income results." Begin to write your own affirmations from your emotions and from your creativity. One of mine is "Now that I am all grown up, I give myself permission to create outstanding results." Another is "I deserve to receive collaborators who edify my gifts and innate talents." One more is "I acknowledge and appreciate my ability to create change in my life and in my enterprise. I am emotionally resilient." It does not matter whose affirmations you use, or if they are worded perfectly. What matters is that you create anchors you can use and believe in to assist you to become the brilliant leader you are destined to become.

Notes

_____

_____

_____

_____

_____

_____

_____

_____

_____

_____

_____

_____

_____

_____

_____

_____

_____

_____

_____

_____

_____

Notes

13

THE POWER OF PERSONALITY

Great entrepreneurs know that it is impossible to get to the top of the game of life without other people. Operating in a vacuum won't get you there; understanding people and building relationships will. Unless you spend your entrepreneurial career selling coconuts to yourself on an island, you will require other people in your organization and in your circle of influence to create the results you seek. By now you have begun to develop a new awareness of why you do what you do, but to lead you must also be aware of why other people do what they do as well.

Identifying and understanding the four main personality types will greatly enhance your leadership ability because you will have an immediate insight into what motivates each of them. Imagine how much easier it would be to communicate with people if you could identify in a few seconds of conversation what motivates them, the situations they resist, what their hot buttons are, and most importantly, what to listen for to know when they are ready to buy from you or to join your organization. This information is designed to create a foundation for you to do just that!

The Four Personality Types

When you understand the four different personalities, you can start to recognize which one of these personalities is dominant in the person you are interacting with. When you can do this, and understand your dominant personality characteristics as well, it becomes much easier to communicate and create relationships with other people.

To assist you to understand the four personalities, Jeff and I have compared them to animals—lions, owls, monkeys, and koalas. Our "lion," the king of the jungle, is a classic type "A" personality. This personality type wants to cut right to the chase, get to the point, and go produce. Our "owl" is the analytical thinker of society and focuses on facts, figures, logic, and order. Our "monkey" loves to socialize and have fun! A monkey is often vivacious and exuberant and not only brings life to any party, he or she often *is* the party. Finally, we have our "koala," the amiable relater and nurturer of society. These are the types of people who are interested in how they can assist others and will often make an emotional decision based on their feelings about you. The point is that it's very important that you are aware and understand on what to say and what to listen for from the different personality temperaments.

The Lion

The lion is the doer of the personality temperaments, aptly known as the king of the jungle. With this personality, you have to cut to the chase, because they're going to interrupt you and say, "What is this about? Can't you just give me some information?" Their motto is, "Get it done," and they want it done yesterday. When it comes to results, they want them now. This is the type of personality temperament that knows how to quickly size up a situation, check in with their emotions, and make quick decisions often acting on their intuition.

Lions can be very impatient, and they like to control people and situations. Don't be surprised if they interrupt you, and don't be afraid to stand up to the lion because this is how you gain the lion's respect. Our lion loves to be the center of attention and thrives on challenges and competition. Someone with this personality type is an extremely high achiever with good administrative skills, and you definitely want this personality temperament in your business because these are the top producers in free enterprise.

Lions are self-starters and self-sufficient and will not require a lot of your time. They are true leaders and are constantly dissatisfied with the status quo. They seek variety, the unusual, the unique, and most of all, the adventurous and exciting. Lions are results-oriented, they love to produce, and they are focused on bottom-line results. Their pace is fast, they operate well under pressure, and they have little to no patience with delays. A lion will always have an opinion, which is generally well formed, and will be quick to express it.

When speaking to this person, you must be direct, positive, and blunt and be willing to cut to the chase, getting to the point of your dialogue in thirty to ninety seconds. Lions have the shortest attention span of any of the personality types and will check out of the conversation if you lose their attention. Do not be intimidated by this personality. Learn to read this person very clearly, because this type of personality can juggle more businesses and more happenings than any other of the personality temperaments.

Lions are also very demanding of themselves and others. They're very susceptible to stress and adrenal burnout. This type of personality will stay on the phone all day, dialing for dollars. They're tremendous in a crisis climate, very closed-minded, and they will ask you, "What can you do for me that others can't?" Lions are extremely goal-oriented, will fight for their own way, are at times extremely stubborn, impatient, and tough; this type of personality will definitely get in the ring with you. Lions love confrontation, but will also accept momentary defeat and will get back up on the mat more quickly than of any of the other personality temperaments. So, when speaking to the "Lion, or the king of the jungle, be prepared to get in the ring, but don't back down. This confrontation is not personal; lions will confront you because this is simply the way they play the game of life.

Most of the other personality temperaments become very intimidated the moment our lion unleashes one roar or says one word. When this happens, remember that this is his posture; take a deep breath and be prepared to get to your point quickly. One of the things that the lion definitely will not tolerate is you reading a script or hesitating when you speak. So be prepared. Be ready to just zip right through the information you are presenting, because that's what they're looking for. If you're presenting to the lion in person, jump right in and get to the point. You must be precise, effective, and organized and deliver your information quickly and effectively because they are extremely impulsive.

Remember, the lion is very challenge-oriented. This is one temperament you can definitely take the opportunity away from and watch him chase after you to see what he is missing out on. This person feels the loss of opportunity and wants it more if he feels he cannot have it. When seeking collaboration with lions, stress what's in it for them and how they can affect the company's bottom line. Focus on the lion's goals and on how they are achievable through the opportunity, product, or service you are presenting. Do not exaggerate, because a lion will not hesitate to call you on the carpet when intuition tells them you are full of fluff.

A lion usually produces the biggest results, but one of the downsides of this temperament is that they are the type of person that can often cause you the most problems in your organization. They love to stir things up and often cause a lot of chaos and drama in their relationships. When interacting with this temperament, trust your intuition, get right to the point, and if they start pushing you around and you know it's going nowhere, don't be afraid to let them go. If your intuition says, *This isn't the kind of person I want in my team*, you are absolutely correct, because one of the biggest downsides of the lion's temperament is that often their ego is bigger than their bank account.

The Owl
Unlike the lion, our owl avoids trouble at all costs. Owls are extremely cautious, precise, and organized. Their motto is "Get the facts and get the facts now, then do the research to be sure the facts are right." The desire to be right and have the proof to back them up is one of the owl's hot buttons. They will adapt to situations to avoid conflict; they are very polite but extremely indifferent, often to the point of seeming cold. Owls are very cautious, very conservative, and very diplomatic. This personality type will also interrupt you in midsentence and say, "What is this about?

Can't you give me some information?" They are often perceived by others as very pessimistic, very skeptical, and very rude, because the owl will not hesitate to correct information they perceive as incorrect.

Use your intuition when talking to this person. If you just don't feel that you can go very far, don't be afraid to just let this person go; this is not someone you can challenge to provoke a decision or to incite interest. Owls are planners and organizers, and they proceed in a very orderly, systematic manner. They're precise perfectionists with an extreme attention to detail. They tend to follow established procedures and maintain a neat, organized environment. Do not allow an owl to suck you into a long, detailed discussion, or you will find yourself trapped in this person's analysis for forty-five minutes and then feel exhausted and be ready to go lay down because they are extremely persistent, systematic problem-solvers.

Owls must see things in writing and will not make a decision until all the facts are in. They are in no hurry and feel no urgency to hold onto what they might lose if opportunity passes them by, so give them the facts, figures, and documentation and move on. Their decisions are made logically with very little emotion, and once their mind is set, they are very rigid. Owls are very precise; they want facts, and they make logical decisions. They love charts and graphs. Do not get into long debates with this personality temperament. Study their desires in a logical, practical manner and then give them all the facts, figures, and documentation they deserve to create an intelligent decision. Our owl is the genius of the jungle—more geniuses come out of this temperament than any other personality type. Respect that they will base their decisions on lots of facts and logical evidence, because this is how they operate.

Our owl is the most difficult of all of the animal personalities to bring into your enterprise. This personality will require the most effort and the longest time to decide to follow you or to go in another direction. When an owl does join your team, they can seem to waste your time—but if you can get them to see the benefits and the bigger picture, they will let go of a lot of their rigidity. Remember, you are communicating with the genius of society.

Don't lose your patience and prejudge the owl too quickly; he's just methodically doing his due diligence.

The Monkey

Our social monkey has a tremendous amount of energy and loves to have fun. One of their mottos is "Let's have fun. Let's do it!" They seek applause for greatness and their time frame is usually not going to be your time frame. This is the type of person that will make an emotional decision if they feel good, but their "now" is usually next week or later. Monkeys are typically dreamers, often with very unrealistic goals. They have strong desires for approval and compliments, and they love an audience and groups. They are extremely creative, outgoing, persuasive, friendly, enthusiastic, and spontaneous. They generate and project a tremendous amount of confidence. Monkeys are usually very conversational, and this is one of their "hot buttons." Monkeys are poised and they meet people easily because they are very likeable.

Monkeys act on opinions and hunches and are very connected to their intuition. They also misjudge people because they are compelled to trust freely and easily, and they often make wrong decisions. This type of personality can be very flighty and will often generalize, exaggerate, and disregard facts as they strive to make their opinions and their beliefs prevail. They love to join groups for prestige and love to be on stage. They live for personal recognition and seek attention and approval. Their ego is their biggest hot button, and how you feed it is going to really affect how they perform when you collaborate.

Monkeys enjoy talking, talking, talking, mostly about themselves. This is the type of personality that you can use one word, "Why?" and they'll continue to talk. Their focus is fun, so let them know how, by having fun in your organization, they can make their dreams come true! They are not interested in compensation structures or how-tos; they just want to feel good. This is the experience they seek in life. They are turned on by other energetic people because this exchange of emotional vibration excites them; you want to learn to "turn on your juice" with this personality, because this connection will create the foundation to build your relationship.

Monkeys have tremendous energy, they have great people skills, and they are natural-born salespeople, but they also become unfocused very quickly. You want to learn how to communicate with this personality type because they typically have great contacts and can bring a great circle of influence to you. Through the monkey, you can find tremendous people, and if you can keep them on track, they can be one of the top producers over the long haul.

The Koala

This brings us to the koala, our amiable relater and nurturer of society. This type of personality temperament produces a lot of teachers, social workers, nurses, caregivers, Red Cross workers, and people who are very in touch and in tune with both nature and other people. Koalas are very in tune with the emotions of other people, and they frequently seek the opinions and approval of those in their circle of influence for reassurance. Their time frame for action is often "never," because they want to think situations through and run them by other people to make sure an opportunity feels good for everyone before creating a decision.

Never underestimate the koala or prejudge this personality type's ability to create results, because this type of person also attracts a lot of really great people and is often a silent leader. This type of person leads, not from the front, but from the back, encouraging and nurturing people behind the scenes. They attract a lot of good quality people because they love to be loved. Koalas seek security and belonging, and they are extremely warm, supportive, reliable, and usually softhearted.

But once again, don't prejudge our warm, cuddly "koala bear," because if you box them in sometimes they'll come out of the corner roaring like a lion. This also is not someone you want to challenge, because they are apt to agree with you when you take an opportunity away from them in order to avoid conflict or confrontation. They dislike time frames and deadlines, and they would rather sacrifice personally to maintain peace in their relationships than face confrontational situations. Koalas ask great questions and listen intently to the answers they receive, but they never forget when they perceive someone has wronged them. They will hold a grudge for an extended period of time, are very security conscious, and enjoy stability in their circumstances. They like knowing what to expect, and typically, dislike change.

A koala requires your attempt to support their feelings, because they are very, very feelings-oriented. This is the type of person you definitely want to introduce to another koala in your enterprise, because they would love to find out that there's a stay-at-home mom that's doing phenomenal in your organization. They love to find out about someone who's overcome the odds. Attempt to support their feelings when it comes to being successful in business. Study their personal desires, as well as their business background. Show them that there is very little risk if they partner with you. Most of all, don't rush them into a decision. Like the owl, they don't like to be pressured. Koalas want to receive a lot of guidance. Patience and understanding is the key to connecting with this personality. They speak softly; however, they can carry a big stick, especially when they feel extremely comfortable about you as a leader and your business as the one they can make a difference in.

Understand that this type of personality temperament is never going to be the #1 producer in your business. On the other hand, they will do a lot of behind-the-scenes work for you and for your company. They usually have tremendous energy, they have great contacts and they will greatly assist you just by the people who they know and know of. When you get this type of person into the flow, they will often surprise you, because deep inside, they are tremendous leaders just waiting to happen.

Understand Your Dominate Personality Type

Each of us is really a rainbow, a conglomeration and combination of each personality type. Understanding your dominant personality, how you are perceived by the other personality types, and how to communicate and connect with them will greatly assist you as an entrepreneur. Your dominant personality may also change, depending on the situation you are in. As an entrepreneur, it is imperative you develop great people skills to create the connections which allow people to follow you.

When you can identify and understand the personality types of the people on your team, and when you can understand what motivates them and what stops them in their tracks, it will be much easier to influence them and to collaborate to create results.

Understanding and communicating effectively with the four main personality types is imperative to achieving success. In this 8-CD audio program Jeffery Combs breaks down the four main personality types, explains their hot buttons and their likes and dislikes, and teaches you how to connect and communicate with each personality to eliminate conflict and inspire collaboration!

In this program, you will learn how to:

- Immediately increase your sales and productivity with each personality type by listening and communicating effectively
- Identify the "hot buttons" that motivate each personality type
- Eliminate "personality conflicts" once and for all
- Create rapport at levels you previously thought impossible
- Instantly identify the four basic personality types to create instant cooperation, enthusiasm, and activity!
- Understand your personal behavior patterns as well as those of others!
- Know why people do what they do!

... And discover if you are a Lion, Monkey, Owl, or Koala!

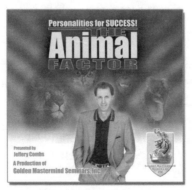

Available online at www.GoldenMastermind.com

Notes

WOMEN IN POWER

Notes

14

YOUR ENTREPRENEURIAL POWER

Since childhood, I have dreamed of being an entrepreneur. My romance with employment began when I was six and told my father I wanted to be a policewoman one morning on our way to the donut shop. My reasoning behind this aspiration the belief that a policewoman would get to go to lots of parties because I had heard about the police breaking up the parties the older kids in high school had on the weekends. By the time I was seven, I realized that policewomen did not make very much money and decided that becoming a psychologist was more in line with the pay scale I would require to live the lifestyle I was already romancing for myself. At nine years of age, I learned how much education this profession required and decided to end my love affair with professional employment. I began to imagine owning a business of my own and being self-employed instead of working for someone else or embarking on a career that required years of education and training. I had no idea what kind of business I wanted to own or how to go about creating one, but I knew without a shadow of a doubt that I wanted to be in charge and make the rules instead of follow the rules someone else had created for me.

Upon reflection, I have realized that reaching this conclusion as a young girl was quite unusual. The idea of owning a business is not unusual, but how was I so certain when I was so young that this was the direction I wanted to go? My mom is an entrepreneur who founded her own veterinary hospital in 1980, when I was three years old. We lived on eight-and-a-half acres in Medina, Ohio where my mom had horses we kept on our property and a garden where we grew almost all of our produce every summer because of my allergies and asthma. My dad worked for the airlines, but he took care of almost all of our property maintenance with my mom's and my assistance when he was home from flying. When he was away on trips, I spent a good deal of my time at my mom's veterinary practice after school. I grew up inside her business and saw from behind the scenes the time, effort and energy required to build a successful business. I also learned a tremendous amount about people and the challenges of having employees. When I was bored, I would pester everyone relentlessly to give me tasks to do so I could be a part of the whole operation.

I learned from both of my parents the power of being independent and self-reliant. My parents are quintessential do-it-yourselfers, and from them I learned basic plumbing, basic woodworking, how to paint a house (and eggshell white was a BORING color to paint!), and how to change the oil in a car. I mowed the lawn, actively assisted in the care of our horses, and generally learned to do as much as possible. I was an only child and my parents became my mentors for many areas of life. My point here is that at a very young age I was learning life skills that created a different sense of self-reliance and independence for me than most of my peers. I learned an entirely different set of decision-making skills than other children, because airline pilots are great critical thinkers and are trained to make decisions with confidence, and veterinarians often face emergency situations that require split-second decisions in the moment when an animal is hovering between life and death, as well as intuitional decisions in the every day practice of veterinary medicine.

As a teenager, I was often told I was thirteen going on thirty; I longed to be an adult so I could have the freedom life had to offer. When I was fifteen, I began my first job as a hostess in our local Perkins. I graduated to a waitress position the following year, so I worked weekends during the school year and kept a full-time schedule in the summer. I had always worked for an allowance from my parents, but this job gave me the opportunity to earn my own money, and I did not have to pass room inspection for my paychecks any longer!

As a waitress, I also had my first experience of receiving compensation for my service in cash. And I learned very quickly that the better my service, the bigger my compensation. The word *tip* is an acronym for "to insure promptness," but waiting tables is a people business and there is a psychology to being a great server. I quickly mastered the art of influencing my customers to tip generously, and they were happy to do so because I transitioned from an order-taker to creating a dining experience for them. I developed a regular clientele and by my senior year, my section was full of repeat diners who requested me every Saturday and Sunday morning. On average I would work sixteen to nineteen hours a weekend and would create more revenue in those mornings than many of my peers would generate in a regular job.

I remained in the service industry for many years and waited tables in many different restaurants ranging from Perkins to five-star establishments. I dallied once in corporate America and learned after less than one year that I did not belong in that arena. I simply did not want to be at the mercy of a boss' rules and regulations in exchange for a paycheck. I was introduced to network marketing in 2001 after spending three years in the direct sales industry. I saw an opportunity to establish my own enterprise with a relatively minimal investment and decided to capitalize on it. Through this company, I heard of Jeffery Combs, and the rest is history. Network marketing was not my final destination, but served me very well as a springboard toward attracting Jeffery to my life, then developing a speaking career, and now becoming an author.

The Power of Your Story

Your entrepreneurial power lies in your personal story. It lies in the challenges and triumphs you have experienced thus far in your journey, provided you are open and share your story with the people seeking to connect with you. Your past experiences do not define you, but they definitely do build character. Every blade of grass you have walked upon has contributed to you reading this very information. The people you seek to attract to you will respect your character and your intestinal fortitude if you will share these experiences with them.

I know that personally when I am seeking a leader, a mentor, or receiving information from another speaker, I want to know where their journey has taken them. I want to know if this person is teaching theory based on outside information or sharing insights and keys to transformation based on personal experience. Every successful person has lived through challenges and triumphs. This is one of the laws of success. I am always more interested in what someone else has done when the chips are down and the odds appear stacked against them than I am in what they are doing now that they have succeeded. I want to learn how someone else had addressed the same challenges I have faced or am currently facing to receive information to ease my transition into the solution. Your story is a key component of your entrepreneurial power.

It is not necessary to be creating huge financial results for your story to be effective. You can be a novice in your industry and your story can still create an impact. This past weekend I shared the same story about my past relationships and how I attracted Jeff to my reality that I shared with you to illustrate to my audience the power of one decision and the power of consciously creating experiences rather than settling for life's circumstances. This one decision is why this book exists in your reality because without that event, this information would never be recorded. Your success will require you to apply the knowledge and skills you gained while transitioning from struggle to ease and from challenges to triumphs, but you do not have to have created massive results in return for this application before others can identify with you and learn from your wisdom.

It is our story that creates the human connection that people are so desperately seeking. This is what it means to connect from the heart. As humans, we have a tendency to feel that someone we perceive as more successful than we are must not have been through the same pain that we have. We project an idealistic reality upon them due to our own doubts about our abilities and our past conditioning. If you can become more objective in these situations and realize that, as humans, we all experience pain and we all desire to be accepted and to receive approval, it will greatly assist you to narrow the gap in your perception of what separates you from the winners in life.

Know Your Purpose

Another key to stepping into your entrepreneurial power is to begin to acknowledge and become comfortable with your emotional purpose for seeking success. Why do you play the game? Are you playing for recognition? Are you playing because you are so psychologically unemployable that this is the only arena where other people understand and accept you? Perhaps you are playing to create an impact on society through the results you achieve. Whatever the reason, we all come to the game seeking emotional fulfillment. Once again, this fulfillment usually comes through our relationships and interactions with other people.

Know What Drives You

It is not always possible to receive this through our relationships in our enterprises, and it is important that you learn to turn to the source which will provide what you seek, rather than return to a source which cannot meet your emotional requirements. For instance, if you have never received approval from one of your parents, then this is probably not the best person to go to when you seek edification of your accomplishments in your enterprise. Instead, go to the person who does acknowledge your brilliance and will give you the encouragement you seek when sharing your results. Knowing where to turn requires being conscious of your requirements. The following list will assist you to begin searching for the answer to your why.

What drives you?

I Want to Be:	So I Receive:
Accepted	Certainty
Included	Recognition
Respected	Power
Prosperous	Abundance
Appreciated	Recognition
Productive	Freedom
Understood	Approval
Loved	Fulfillment

Take a few moments to create a list for yourself, and then narrow your list to the three most critical situations for you. Consider where your emotional requirements are currently being met. Are they met in ways that fuel you or in ways that create challenges for you? Your list will change as you grow and develop, but it will always require boundaries to ensure that you recognize when your requirements are being infringed upon by others. When this happens and you do not feel fulfilled, free enterprise become a struggle and can be painful instead of empowering.

For example, this means addressing a situation when you feel you are not receiving the respect you deserve from a colleague, so you can communicate how you feel and how the situation can change before you are so overwhelmed by your emotions that the situation results in conflict. The only way you can learn to express your requirements and communicate effectively is by realizing you are approaching a state of emotional deficit before you become emotionally and spiritually bankrupt. With repetition, this becomes a new method of operation and then becomes a habit. When you are in the habit of effectively communicating how you expect others to treat you, you will be amazed at how powerful you feel and how easily you are able to empower others.

A Constant Evolution

We all carry emotional luggage from our past with us on our entrepreneurial journey, but the weight of that baggage is entirely up to each of us to decide. Entrepreneurial power lies in understanding your past and how it affects your present, as well as learning to release and neutralize the emotions which no longer serve you as you strive to achieve new objectives. It also lies in your ability to share your vulnerabilities with others and to tell your story and how you have developed as a result of your experiences to allow others to connect with you and feel your value. Once again, this is a process, not a payoff.

YOUR ENTREPRENEURIAL POWER

Free enterprise is a game of constant evolution and transformation. Welcome to the game! I commend you for having the courage to grow and to change, as well as to take bigger risks as you begin to receive bigger rewards. I look forward to connecting with you and to celebrating your journey when we meet on the campus of life.

Notes

_____
_____
_____
_____
_____
_____
_____
_____
_____
_____
_____
_____
_____
_____
_____
_____
_____
_____
_____
_____

Notes

Erica Combs

Erica Combs is the vice president of Golden Mastermind Seminars, Inc. and an internationally recognized speaker, author, and trainer. Her experience in free enterprise combined with her personal growth has allowed her to step into her power and assist her clients to reconnect with their power and brilliance to create quantum changes in their enterprises and in their lives!

Based upon her personal experience, Erica can assure you firsthand that success as an entrepreneur requires an entirely different level of self-esteem, communication, focus and permission than most people are taught is acceptable by their families, coworkers, and peers. Success will require that you begin to examine your current beliefs and give yourself permission to release those which no longer serve you so that you may adopt new and empowering beliefs to lead you to manifesting your dreams.

Erica's coaching and training focuses on creating a foundation for you to begin your journey to personal power, and to create an anchor you can use to reconnect with your internal peace as you continue your journey of personal development in the land of free enterprise.

Erica is available for consulting, mentoring, and personal one-on-one coaching. Her professional guidance will assist you to create maximum results now! Erica doesn't teach theory - she teaches the same skills she uses in business so you can begin creating the results you desire in free enterprise today!

For further information, please call 800-595-6632 or visit her website at www.GoldenMastermind.com.

Golden Mastermind Seminars, Inc.

President & CEO of Golden Mastermind Seminars, Inc.

Internationally recognized trainer in the network marketing & direct sales industry and keynote speaker

Has personally coached and consulted with thousands of entrepreneurs and industry leaders since retiring as a ten-year veteran marketer

Committed to assisting people to change the way they feel in order to achieve their goals and dreams

Specializes in a 2-1/2 day workshop called Breakthroughs to Success! This is an absolute must for anyone desiring to go to the next level

Jeffery Combs

FREE

"More Heart Than Talent" Teleconference training call with Erica & Jeffery Combs every Tuesday night

Time: 10:30 pm EST
Call: 212-461-5860 / PIN 7707#

800-595-6632
www.GoldenMastermind.com

BREAKTHROUGHS TO SUCCESS

A 2½ Day Intensive Personal Growth &
Entrepreneurial Retreat Featuring Jeffery & Erica Combs
Location: Stockton, CA

Breakthroughs Exercises:

- The Psychology of Wealth
- Letting Go of Your Ego!
- Emotional Healing
- Getting Money Right Emotionally
- Forgiveness
- Being in the Moment

Breakthroughs To Success will assist you to breakthrough and heal the emotional barriers that have kept you from achieving the level of success you deserve in your enterprise. Spend 2½ empowering days with Jeffery & Erica Combs in a small, private setting.

Receive luxury transportation to and from the Sacramento airport via limousine service, catered lunches, and hands-on training with Jeff & Erica!

Release Your Limitations & Discover The Power of Belief!

YOU DESERVE TO HAVE IT ALL!

800-595-6632
www.GoldenMastermind.com

Notes

_____
_____
_____
_____
_____
_____
_____
_____
_____
_____
_____
_____
_____
_____
_____
_____
_____
_____
_____
_____
_____
_____
_____
_____
_____
_____

Notes

_____
_____
_____
_____
_____
_____
_____
_____
_____
_____
_____
_____
_____
_____
_____
_____
_____
_____
_____
_____

Notes

_____
_____
_____
_____
_____
_____
_____
_____
_____
_____
_____
_____
_____
_____
_____
_____
_____
_____
_____
_____
_____
_____
_____
_____

WOMEN IN POWER

Notes

_____
_____
_____
_____
_____
_____
_____
_____
_____
_____
_____
_____
_____
_____
_____
_____
_____
_____
_____
_____
_____
_____
_____
_____
_____
_____